Is Self-Determination a Dangerous Illusion?

Political Theory Today

David Miller

———————

Is Self-Determination a Dangerous Illusion?

polity

First published in 2020 by Polity Press

Polity Press
65 Bridge Street
Cambridge CB2 1UR, UK

Polity Press
101 Station Landing
Suite 300
Medford, MA 02155, USA

ISBN-13: 978-1-5095-3346-6
ISBN-13: 978-1-5095-3347-3 (pb)

A catalogue record for this book is available from the British Library.

Library of Congress Cataloging-in-Publication Data
Names: Miller, David, 1946- author.
Title: Is self-determination a dangerous illusion? / David Miller.
Description: Medford, MA : Polity, 2019. | Series: Political theory today
Identifiers: LCCN 2019014896 (print) | LCCN 2019981425 (ebook) |
    ISBN 9781509533466 (hardback) | ISBN 9781509533473 (pbk.) | ISBN
    9781509533497 (ebook)
Subjects: LCSH: Self-determination, National.
Classification: LCC KZ1269 .M55 2019 (print) | LCC KZ1269 (ebook) |
    DDC 341.26--dc23
LC record available at https://lccn.loc.gov/2019014896
LC ebook record available at https://lccn.loc.gov/2019981425

Typeset in 11 on 15 Sabon
by Fakenham Prepress Solutions, Fakenham, Norfolk NR21 8NL
Printed and bound in the UK by CPI Group (UK) Ltd, Croydon

For further information on Polity, visit our website: politybooks.com

Contents

v

Acknowledgements

This book was written in the delightful surroundings of the Institute for Futures Studies in Stockholm, where visitors have no specific obligations other than to meet occasionally for *fika* to consume coffee and *kanelbullar*. I should like to thank Gustaf Arrhenius, Ludvig Beckman and the staff of the Institute for the support they provided, and for stimulating conversations on topics more or less closely related to self-determination. Material from the book was presented there and also to political theory workshops at Uppsala University and Nuffield College, Oxford: I am very grateful to everyone who offered comments and made suggestions at those meetings. Thanks are due, too, to George Owers and three readers for Polity Press for providing detailed comments on the manuscript, in the process saving me from a number of *faux pas*. Last but not least, Margaret has been a constant source of advice and encouragement.

1

Introduction

In 1976, the United Nations re-affirmed its commitment to human rights in two major documents, the *International Covenant on Civil and Political Rights* and the *International Covenant on Economic, Social and Cultural Rights*. Both contained, as Article 1, the following sentences: 'All peoples have the right of self-determination. By virtue of that right they freely determine their political status and freely pursue their economic, social and cultural development.'

The presence of this Article is puzzling in several respects. It seems out of place in documents devoted to setting out a long list of individual human rights since the right it proclaims is clearly a collective right, a right belonging to peoples, plural, not to individual persons, as the Article's wording makes plain. During the long period in which

1

the Covenants were being drafted, several western governments had opposed its inclusion, no doubt foreseeing the implications it would have for their remaining colonial possessions. Then there is the initially surprising fact that no attempt is made to clarify the term 'people'. If 'people' isn't just another word for 'state', who counts as one and who doesn't? Nor does the Article explain what self-determination involves. The second sentence suggests two things: that a 'people' should decide on how it wants to organize itself politically, such as by having its own independent state; and that it should then set its own domestic policy goals. But the Article does not require that it must adopt a democratic form of government. As we shall see later, self-determination and democracy, though they are related, are not the same. By placing self-determination at the head of a long list of human rights, the Covenants imply that a people is being seriously wronged if denied the right to govern itself but give us little clue as to what following Article 1 might mean in practice.

International lawyers have struggled to clarify this alleged right of self-determination. A narrow interpretation would say that it is simply intended to protect established states from external inter-ference. In other words, a 'people' is indeed nothing more or less than a state. But in practice it has been interpreted more widely than this so as to apply in two main cases where newly independent states are being created. One of these is decolonization of the kind that occurred in the 1960s and 1970s, when European states were forced to relinquish their possessions in Africa and Asia. In this context, the inhabitants of former colonies were treated as separate 'peoples' with a right to break free from their colonial masters and found independent states. The other is the collapse of large conglomerates, such as occurred at the end of the First World War when the Habsburg and Ottoman Empires were dissolved. Here, new states, such as Poland and Czechoslovakia, were created in order to grant self-government to nations who had been submerged in the former empires but were now given the right to control their own destinies.[1]

This indeed was the moment at which the idea of self-determination first sprang to prominence. It was supported for different reasons by the Bolsheviks under Lenin's leadership and by US President Woodrow Wilson, who played a large part in redrawing the map of Europe in an attempt to ensure that state borders and national borders would henceforth coincide. Wilson announced as his fundamental principle:

that the countries of the world belong to the people who live in them, and that they have a right to determine their own destiny and their own form of government and their own policy, and that no body of statesmen, sitting anywhere, no matter whether they represent the overwhelming physical force of the world or not, has the right to assign any great people to a sovereignty under which it does not care to live.[2]

But how could this bold claim be put into practice? It appears to assume that 'countries' are made up of people who, once given the chance, would all agree on how they wish to be governed, so the problem of self-determination could be solved by going and asking them the question directly. But what if, instead, we find that, in Europe and elsewhere, populations are interspersed in such a way that it is impossible to draw neat boundaries around them and say that we have found homogeneous 'peoples' who are then entitled, by Wilson's principle, to choose their form of government? Then it seems that achieving self-determination for one nation will involve denying it to others, who might form a minority within the borders of one country, or be dispersed across two or more. Wilson's Secretary of State, Robert Lansing, who was closely involved in the post-war peace negotiations, came to regard his master's pronouncement with dismay:

> The more I think about the President's declaration as to the right of 'self-determination', the more convinced I am of the danger of putting such ideas into the minds of certain races. It is bound to be the basis of impossible demands on the Peace Congress and create trouble in many lands. . . . The phrase is simply loaded with dynamite. It will raise hopes which can never be realised. It will, I fear, cost thousands of lives. . . . What a calamity that the phrase was ever uttered! What misery it will cause![3]

From the examples he offers, it appears that Lansing's main concern was the encouragement that Wilson's doctrine would offer to groups already struggling against their inclusion in colonial empires or large states, and so the violence that he anticipated would occur because the imperial powers would forcefully resist their demands. But Lansing worried too that some self-determination claims might simply be mutually incompatible. If the Boers were granted self-determination within South Africa, how could the other peoples of that region enjoy it too? Or if the Jews were to achieve self-determination in Palestine, as Wilson's commitment to Zionism implied, what would become of the Arab inhabitants of that area? Lansing's words were prophetic indeed; and they give us one very obvious sense in which self-determination might be a dangerous illusion. Proclaiming self-determination as a human right suggests that it is something that every human being can enjoy, like the right to food or bodily security. But what if the self-determination of some is always achieved at the expense of the self-determination of others?

The problem Lansing identified is not the only reason for thinking that self-determination might be a dangerous illusion – that by leading people to hope for something it may be impossible for them to achieve, it opens the door to resentment, political alienation and, in the worst case, violence. Although I will argue in this book in favour of the moral and political importance of self-determination, I want to take the case against it seriously as well. Let me add to Lansing's criticism three more reasons for doubting that collective self-determination is a political goal worth pursuing.

The first takes us back to the silence of the International Covenants on the question of who counts as a people for purposes of self-determination. Is there any non-arbitrary way of deciding which groups should be given the right to govern themselves? To confine the right of self-determination to existing *states* is effectively to say that only those who have already achieved self-determination are entitled to exercise it. But this makes little sense, morally speaking. How could we justify saying that once the Estonians had their own state, they were entitled to be self-determining, but so long as they were part of the Soviet Union they were not? As we have already seen, international law, despite the fact that its principles tend to reflect the interests of established states, has also recognized self-determination rights in two main cases where groups did not already have their own states. But if we now compare these cases more closely, we see that their underlying logic is somewhat contradictory. In the aftermath of the First World War, when new independent states were being created, their boundaries were drawn broadly along national lines. For instance, a Polish state was created to grant self-determination to the Polish nation, a people united by ties of language, culture and religion, with a territorial heartland and a history of political independence that had rudely been brought to an end in 1795 when their state was partitioned between Austria, Prussia and Russia. So here the relevant 'people' was defined first, in terms of national identity, and then the territorial boundaries of their vehicle of self-determination – the state – were drawn so as to encase it geographically.

In the period of decolonization following the Second World War, by contrast, a very different logic was followed. The process was governed by the international legal principle of *uti possidetis*, which holds that where new state borders are being defined, they must follow existing lines of demarcation between administrative units.[4] But, as many commentators have pointed out, colonial boundaries were created for different purposes and often as a result of mutually advantageous deals struck between the colonizers, so the areas they circumscribe were unlikely to be suitable as the territories of independent states. Indeed, internal boundary lines within colonies may have been drawn with the intention of keeping the colony intact by cutting across the territories traditionally held by different ethnic groups, but that became a source of problems once these smaller units became independent.[5] The aftermath of decolonization left many ethnic groups in the position of national minorities who were denied their own rights of self-determination and, in consequence, very often many other rights as well. Colonial domination was replaced by domination by the majority ethnic group in the newly independent state.

In the earlier period and the European context, then, the 'peoples' who were considered ripe for self-determination were historic nations defined mainly in ethno-cultural terms; while in the later period and the post-colonial context, the relevant 'peoples' were those who lived within pre-existing administrative borders, regardless of their ethno-cultural affinities, or lack of them. The first way of understanding peoplehood might appear superior to the second because less arbitrary, but no one should imagine that the world is made up of neat, consolidated nations potentially able to live within boundaries drawn in such a way that everyone inside is a compatriot (even Iceland, potentially a good candidate, now contains nearly a tenth of its population who are not native-born Icelanders). Often we find that people with contrasting national identities are geographically interspersed over wide areas, so there is no way of drawing clean lines between national communities; or else we find smaller nations 'nested' inside larger ones, as the Scots and the Welsh are in Britain, and the Catalans and Basques are in Spain, and the question is whether the right of self-determination is held primarily by the encompassing group or the sub-group. There is no obvious answer, and in practice the issue may be settled by the exercise of power, as happened in 2017, for instance, when the Spanish state forcibly suppressed Catalan demands for independence.

There is already a hint of this problem in Woodrow Wilson's statement granting rights of sovereignty to 'any *great* people' (my italics). But why not to *little* people as well (or instead)? Wilson helped to achieve self-determination for the Poles, at least for a time, but there was no such opportunity for the three million or so Ukrainians who lived inside the new Polish state, or for the Silesians, who initially were only allowed to choose, in a plebiscite, between joining Poland and joining Germany. After three violent insurrections, a partition of Silesia between the two states was agreed. But self-determination for the Silesians themselves was never considered.

The point can be put more abstractly: no one is ever in a position to choose all of their fellow citizens, the people with whom they could potentially exercise a right of self-determination. This applies even on a small scale. Each of us can choose whom we want to have as friends, but there's no guarantee that our own friends will also befriend one another. Society doesn't divide itself up into neat friendship circles within which everyone loves everyone else. Scale this up to the size of a modern state, and the problem is obvious. We have to share a political home with people, many of whom we'd prefer to avoid associating with if we could. So no way of sorting people into political groups for purposes of self-determination is going to satisfy everyone. In which case, the critics argue, what does all the fuss about self-determination amount to? Let's return to the Catalonia/Spain case. Suppose Catalonia does indeed become an independent state, and consider the position of any Catalan taken at random. She now finds herself in political association with some 5.5 million Catalans instead of the 36.5 million Spaniards she consorted with before. Apart from the independence issue itself, her new associates will be just as diverse in terms of moral beliefs, lifestyle choices, tastes in art and music, political ideology, and so forth as the ones she had previously. Finding a way to live together under a common political roof is no easier now than it ever was. So what, a critic will ask, has really been gained?

I have so far considered two charges against the idea of self-determination. The first is that self-determination claims inevitably conflict: self-determination for group A comes at the expense of self-determination for group B because, for example, A wants to exercise control over territory that members of B also occupy. The second is that self-determination claims are arbitrary because there is no objective way of defining the relevant 'self'. People will inevitably prefer different ways of slicing up the world into separate political communities, but none of these is unequivocally the best. So changing the present configuration, whether by breaking up existing states, amalgamating them, or altering their boundaries, could never be worth the disruption it causes. These charges clearly deserve a reply, but rather than attempt this now I want to consider a third reason why self-determination might be a dangerous illusion.

This is that self-determination claims greatly exaggerate the extent to which any 'people' in today's interconnected world are able to control their own destiny. Of course, there are certain questions that can indeed be freely decided within a political community. You can vote on whether to remain a constitutional monarchy or to become a republic with an elected or appointed head of state, as Australians did in 1999. You can vote on whether to replace the national flag with a new flag that is more representative of the way the country now sees itself, as New Zealanders did in 2016 (in each case the result was 'no change'). But these are primarily cultural or symbolic questions with little material effect on people's lives. When it comes to larger economic, social and even many cultural issues, however, nominally independent states find themselves tightly constrained by global forces. They cannot stray far from orthodox neo-liberal economic policies without finding themselves punished through capital flight, currency devaluation, or International Monetary Fund (IMF) intervention. Social policy is similarly constrained by the need to keep taxes low and public borrowing within strict limits so that overseas investors do not take fright. Even preserving local cultures becomes difficult once cultural material of every kind is available through the internet, unless the state is allowed to impose quite severe restrictions on people's freedom of choice and expression.

Concrete illustrations of this problem are easy to find. Consider Greece's attempt to escape from economic austerity in 2015. Following the election of a government headed by the left-wing party Syriza in January, a referendum was held in July in which the voters were asked whether to accept a bailout package proposed jointly by the European Commission, the IMF and the European Central Bank. In return for being granted yet more relief on its accumulated debt, the government would undertake to reduce public expenditure still further. The Greek electorate rejected the package by 61 percent to 39 percent. Yet, faced with the prospect of being ejected from the Eurozone (or even possibly from the European Union itself), the Syriza government rapidly backtracked, accepted the bailout and imposed further harsh austerity measures on top of those already in place. Unemployment levels rose, poverty levels rapidly increased and social services were drastically cut back.

The situation facing Greece was certainly made worse by its unwise earlier decision to join the euro in circumstances in which its economy was not sufficiently aligned with those of countries in the north of Europe to make a common currency viable. It nonetheless plainly demonstrates how self-determination, in the economic sphere, can readily be thwarted by the limited options that the global economy, together with international institutions such as the European Union, makes available. In the Greek case, the choice was essentially between austerity and economic collapse. Those who voted 'No' in the referendum must have imagined there was a third alternative, but probably there wasn't in the circumstances they were facing. Economic isolation – severing all lines of international trade and investment – although possible in theory is extremely costly in practice. Who wants to be North Korea?

For a cultural example, admittedly a much less momentous one, consider Icelanders' attempt to preserve the purity of their native language, which has remained largely unchanged since the composition of the famous Sagas in the twelfth century CE. To prevent its corruption by imported foreign terms, they have steadfastly pursued a policy of creating Icelandic words as required when new technologies and so forth appear. Language is central to Icelandic national identity. But because it is only spoken by between three and four hundred thousand people worldwide, there is little incentive on the part of designers of computer programmes and others in the technology sector to create Icelandic language software. So children, who now acquire much of their vocabulary from their tablets and iPhones, are becoming more fluent in English than in Icelandic.[6] Thus, despite the best intentions of the Icelanders themselves, Icelandic might in the space of a generation or two decline from being the language of common use to being something more like a hobby language used only by purists. This is not the result of anyone's conscious design but merely the unintended consequence of the economics of computer programming.

The third charge, then, is that self-determination is an illusion because political communities have far less scope for choice than their members believe. This is rarely because their decisions will be deliberately blocked by other states. More frequently, their attempt to implement what they have decided is rendered ineffective by global factors over which nobody in particular has any control. And the illusion may become dangerous if the effect is to make citizens lose faith in democratic politics. Politicians present themselves to the electorate with programmes that they claim they will carry out if given the mandate to do so. Yet, once in government, they often appear unable to deliver on what they had promised. This may be for reasons of the kind suggested by the two examples I have given. The politicians may be wholly sincere in their attempt to implement the policies contained in their election manifestos. There is, for example, no reason to think that the Greek Prime Minister Alexis Tsipras was not perfectly sincere when he fought and won the January 2015 election on an anti-austerity platform, or when he later campaigned for a 'No' vote in the referendum on the proposed Greek bailout. But when confronting Greece's creditors directly, he presumably came to the conclusion that there was no feasible alternative to accepting the terms they were now offering. However, voters might well conclude that he never really meant what he had told them beforehand, leading to disillusion, or worse. Why vote, if the person you are about to vote for is never actually going to deliver on her promises? It is then tempting to look towards the strongman who vows that he will do whatever it takes to promote the country's interests against the outside world. To accomplish this, he insists that various democratic constraints on the leader's power – such as term limits on the holding of office – must be removed. In the name of self-determination, democracy may begin to slide towards authoritarianism.

This brings us directly to the question of how self-determination and democracy are related. That they are not identical can be seen most easily by returning to the example of Catalonia and Spain. Spain is obviously a representative democracy in the same sense as many other European states, and a resident of Barcelona with Spanish citizenship cannot complain that she is being governed undemocratically, especially when significant decision powers are devolved to city level. But if she is a Catalan nationalist, she will claim that she is being denied self-determination. Her complaint is not about the mechanics of decision making in general but about the political unit within which decisions are being taken, which, she believes in her case, ought primarily to be Catalonia rather than Spain. The broader point is that democracy can operate once the boundaries of the political unit have been settled – once the 'self' in self-determination has been fixed. There is no overarching democratic procedure for fixing those boundaries, however: as Sir Ivor Jennings famously remarked, 'On the surface [the doctrine of self-determination] seemed reasonable: let the people decide. It was in fact ridiculous because the people cannot decide until somebody decides who are the people'.[7] Who should decide whether Catalonia becomes an independent state or remains a semi-autonomous region of Spain? If we say 'the Catalans themselves', we beg the question in one way, while if we say 'the whole of Spain', we beg it in another.

So self-determination is more than democracy because it requires that the unit within which democratic procedures – like voting in elections – are going to operate should be constituted so that as far as possible all and only the relevant 'people' are included within it. One of the tasks ahead is to spell out how this should be done. But is it also less than democracy? Could self-determination be achieved even though the political system is not democratic? In principle it seems so. Suppose government is placed in the hands of a person or a small group who are widely recognized to embody the priorities and values of the society. Think of the religious leadership of a country where the vast majority of people are devout. The people cannot control what their leaders do, yet because they view them as representing their own interests and values, they feel no lack of self-determination. But are they self-determining in fact?

I will postpone that question as well in order to introduce the fourth critical challenge to the idea of self-determination. Assume for now that the procedure for reaching political decisions is indeed democratic, for if there are problems with self-determination in this case it seems very likely they will recur in the absence of democracy. The challenge is that, for self-determination to be of value, it is not enough that there is some mechanism by means of which people are able to make political decisions (such as voting in elections or referendums). The decisions themselves must be of a certain quality: they must at least be sufficiently rational and sufficiently coherent. Would it count as (valuable) self-determination if citizens repeatedly voted for policies that were not in their interests, or voted today for a policy that simply undermined or reversed the policy they had voted for yesterday?

We need to ask why self-determination might fail in this way. One reason is that people are simply very poor at making political decisions. They are badly informed about the issues at stake, and even when factually informed cannot get their heads around complex issues, particularly those involving statistical probabilities – small risks of very bad outcomes, for example. There is plenty of evidence that supports this pessimistic view of the political capacities of the ordinary citizen.[8] Of course, this might change if people were given more opportunity to participate in decisions that were really significant to them. But this would still leave two other concerns we might have about the internal mechanics of self-determination.

The first is that the idea of self-determination conjures up the idea of a unified people all moving in the same direction towards a common goal. But what if people simply disagree about the destination? In that case, presumably, there will have to be some form of majority decision making. But then the question is whether this still grants self-determination to the minority. We have seen that simply being part of a democratic system can't be sufficient for self-determination, otherwise the

Catalonia/Spain issue could never arise. So how can self-determination extend to the dissenting minority, who may accept the boundaries of the political unit but deeply object to the direction in which it is currently travelling? Self-determination claims are sometimes expressed as demands that 'the will of the people' should be respected. But is there really any such thing, and, if there isn't, how can the right of self-determination embrace everyone inside the political community?[9]

The second concern is that even if 'the will of the people' is usually in practice 'the will of the majority of people', that too may prove elusive in certain cases. This is most easily explained through an example.[10] In early 2019, there was a heated debate over whether a second referendum should be held on the United Kingdom's decision to leave the European Union (EU). Those who favoured having one recognized that there was a problem about what the question on the ballot paper ought to be. Broadly speaking, there were three main options facing the country. The first was to reverse the earlier decision and remain in the EU. The second was to accept an agreement with the EU that kept the United Kingdom largely aligned with European legislation on trade in goods and services – the so-called 'soft Brexit' option. The third was for the United Kingdom to leave without a deal and operate under World Trade Organization rules – the so-called 'hard Brexit' option. There was substantial public support for each of these proposals, which suggests that all three ought to be included on the referendum ballot paper. But, if so, how would we decide what the public has voted for when the numbers are in?

There are several ways of solving this problem. One is simply to adopt the option that has attracted most votes. But would that necessarily represent 'the will of the majority'? Suppose that in the case we are discussing, 'Remain' got most votes but less than 50 per cent. But suppose also that almost everyone who voted for 'soft Brexit' would prefer *any* kind of Brexit to 'Remain' and the same was true of those who had voted for 'hard Brexit'. Could we still say that 'Remain' was the people's choice? Another possibility would be to eliminate the option the attracted fewest votes first time round and have a run-off vote between the two that are left in play (presidential elections often work like this). Yet another method would be to invite the voters to rank the three options and award each option two points whenever it came first in someone's ranking and one point whenever it came second, then total up all the points awarded. Each of these methods has arguments in its favour, but in the circumstances described they may well yield different results, none of which can be presented unequivocally as 'what the people have decided'. Nor is it possible to choose between them 'democratically' – the same problem recurs.

So alongside the worry that the minority may be excluded from self-determination when decisions are made by majority vote, we now have the worry that even 'the will of the majority' may be an artificial creation of the voting system in use. This carries with it a number of further dangers, such as inconsistency over time between the decisions that are said to represent such a will.

I began this chapter on a positive note by citing international covenants in which self-determination is hailed as a human right. Then I explored four reasons why we might think of it as a dangerous illusion: the self-determination claims of different 'peoples' may collide; there might be no non-arbitrary way of deciding who counts as a 'people' in the first place; in an interconnected world, the scope for practising self-determination may be very narrow; and finally, the idea that a people share a common will which they express through their political decisions is mostly a myth. All of this looks like bad news for the idea of self-determination. Should we then just abandon it? In the rest of the book, I will attempt a modest rescue operation. I start by asking why we should value self-determination in the first place.

2

The Value of Self-Determination

We saw in the last chapter how important self-determination has become as a political ideal, notwithstanding the many problems that apparently beset it. But we have yet to explain its value. Human beings haven't always cared so much about belonging to self-governing political communities. To be sure, there are famous historical examples of small political groups fighting off large oppressors in the name of freedom: the Athenians and the Spartans defying the might of the Persian Empire, the Scottish nobility declaring at Arbroath in 1320 that 'as long as but a hundred of us remain alive, never will we on any conditions be brought under English rule. It is in truth not for glory, nor riches, nor honours that we are fighting, but for freedom – for that alone, which no honest man gives up but with life itself'.[1] But these are exceptional, albeit inspiring, cases. For most people, most of the time, what matters is the quality of their personal lives: whether they are safe, well fed, healthy and able to live according to their own customs and traditions. Whether they are ruled by this lord or that, one dynasty or another, hasn't generally been important so long as these more basic needs are met.

But this has changed over the past two centuries, in Europe and North America first and the rest of the world subsequently. In almost every place where people are subject to 'alien' rule, independence movements dedicated to self-determination have arisen, some peaceful, some violent. Why have people come to believe that freedom is not only an individual right but a collective right – indeed, that they cannot be truly free as persons unless they belong to a political body which itself is free from outside domination?

Some arguments in favour of self-determination, particularly those where the self is identified with the nation, attribute its value to the collective itself rather than to its individual members. It is claimed, for example, that the nation has a destiny which it must fulfil. Or an organic metaphor is used: a people is like a rare plant which must be given the freedom to grow and blossom in its own special way. But these essentialist arguments are unlikely now to be found convincing, so I will set them aside.[2] I will assume that to defend political self-determination, we must show that it is valuable for the individual people who make up the self. Keep in mind, too, that the task ahead is not simply to justify democracy. It is fairly easy to find reasons why people benefit from living under a democratically elected government, such as the incentive this creates for the government to protect their interests. To defend self-determination itself, we need to be able to show that people not only have good grounds to throw off dictators and colonial oppressors, but that they are also sometimes justified in demanding it from *within* well-functioning democratic states.

Thinking about the value of *individual* self-determination, or autonomy (I shall use these terms interchangeably) can be illuminating here. Why do people have the right to direct their personal lives so long as they do not cause harm to others or disrupt valuable social practices? One obvious reason is that they are likely to be the best judges of their own interests: they are uniquely well-placed to work out what their main goals in life are and how best to pursue them. But this instrumental reason doesn't exhaust the value of autonomy. We have reason to respect people's decisions even when we are convinced they will later come to regret them.

Suppose a friend decides to throw up a good job in order to travel round the world for a year. Knowing her as we do, we think this is a really bad idea. Yet, although we might try to persuade her to reconsider, once it becomes clear that she is determined to go through with her plan, we should not try to prevent her. She is her own person, and we must respect her decision. What the example highlights is that autonomy has *intrinsic* value over and above its instrumental value in enabling us to pursue the goals that are most important to us.

Notice, though, that in valuing individual autonomy, we are implicitly making certain assumptions about the person whose autonomy we are being asked to respect. We assume, for example, that this person is capable of forming reasonably accurate beliefs about the world around him, that he acts on the basis of coherent preferences, and that the decisions he reaches are consistent over time, so that he doesn't merely undo tomorrow what he has decided upon today. Faced with evidence that people don't in fact live up to these standards – for example evidence about how people will choose differently when presented with materially the same options but with a different framing, or about confirmation bias in the formation of beliefs, or about the many other forms of irrationality detected by psychologists

– our commitment to respecting autonomy begins to crumble.[3] We don't, in other words, value the act of choosing entirely for its own sake: we value it in so far as it enables the chooser to develop a consistent life-plan that fulfils her needs and expresses her values. Where choices lead in the other direction, especially towards serious and irreversible self-harm, we are ready to step in and attempt to forestall or redirect them. So the instrumental and intrinsic reasons for valuing self-determination aren't wholly independent of one another: respecting a person only entails respecting the choices they make when these choices advance something we can recognize as a coherent plan of life, even if it's not one that we would choose for ourselves.

This must be kept in mind when we ask whether self-determination for groups is valuable for the same reasons as self-determination for individuals. Recall from the last chapter those critics of self-determination who fear that group decision making might not meet basic standards of coherence and rationality: they will need to be answered in due course. But first we must establish whether it is even possible to extend the case for individual self-determination to apply to groups.

That extension would be easy to make if everyone in the group had the same goal. If each member of a hiking group wants to climb Mount Kilimanjaro, then by giving the whole group the freedom to choose to climb Kilimanjaro together, we also enhance individual self-determination. But that example is deliberately contrived. Most groups are composed of members with partially conflicting aims and priorities. When the group decides collectively on a course of action, some members will be pleased and others dissatisfied with the result. For the latter at least, it is not clear how granting the group self-determination promotes their own.

But perhaps self-determination for groups is intrinsically valuable in the same way as it is for individuals. Recall the argument in the individual case: by allowing people to make self-regarding decisions unhindered, we show respect for them as persons with the capacity to run their own lives. Conversely, when we interfere so as to deny them that opportunity, we are implicitly declaring them incapable of making respect-worthy choices. By analogy, if we refuse to award self-determination rights to groups, we seem to be saying that they lack the capacity to control their own collective lives, at least in a way that complies with minimum standards of rationality. This would also then disrespect the individual members since what the group does is only a composite of what its members do. By labelling the group incompetent, we cannot avoid labelling its individual members incompetent. Conversely, to respect the members individually as autonomous beings, we must acknowledge their *collective* right of self-determination.[4]

This argument looks strongest in cases where denying a right of self-determination clearly conveys a message of disrespect. Colonial rule is the best example since refusing to grant colonized peoples self-determination was often explicitly justified by asserting that their racial or cultural inferiority made them unfit to govern themselves. But it is harder to apply to cases in which people who are already citizens of established democracies seek to exercise a right of self-determination through seceding. Suppose the United Kingdom were to follow the example of the Spanish government and refuse to allow the Scots to hold any further independence referendums. Whatever view you take of that decision, it would be implausible to represent it as disrespecting the Scots by portraying them as incapable of governing themselves. No serious person, not even the most fanatical Unionist, believes that Scotland would be ungovernable as an independent state. Scottish people are recognized as politically competent by being granted the vote, alongside other British citizens, in national and sub-national elections. So their case for independence cannot be made by arguing that they are being disrespected as individuals so long as it is withheld.

An independence supporter might reply here that what is *not* being respected is the wish for independence itself. To simplify matters, take a case where a very large majority of an incorporated group wants to be self-determining. Isn't it disrespectful to deny them what they seek? However, we don't in general disrespect people simply because we refuse to give them what they want. Suppose I am the manager of a football team and my star player very much wants to play up front, scoring goals. Yet I know that for the good of the team, his best position will be central defender. I don't disrespect him when I override his wishes and insist that he plays in defence. By analogy, self-determination claims cannot be built simply on preferences, even when they are widely shared. It isn't enough to say that you (collectively) *want* to be autonomous: you have to explain why it is impermissible for others to deny you the freedom you are asking for. In general, then, and leaving special cases such as decolonization aside, appealing to respect for persons won't explain why groups can claim a right to self-determination.

We need to find another way of moving from individual to collective autonomy.

In making this move, it's helpful to begin with a case where the potentially autonomous group is relatively small and then see whether the argument for granting them self-determination can be extended to large groups such as nations.[5] So imagine a residential street containing many households with children. Currently, the street is rather dangerous for pedestrians since it is regularly used as a cut-through by speeding cars. It would be much better for the residents if the traffic could be slowed by barriers and the street enhanced by planting greenery and creating small areas where children could play. Then think of two ways in which such a plan could be put into effect. The residents themselves could come together and create an association within which they would discuss the pros and cons of various ways forward, eventually deciding, perhaps after a vote, on a blueprint for humanizing their street. Alternatively, a local official could be sent to ask the residents for their views, perhaps administering a questionnaire, after which the official would propose a development plan. Why might we think that the first alternative, which embodies local self-determination, is better than the second?

We might believe the neighbours stand a better chance of getting the street design that most of them prefer by taking the matter into their own hands. But suppose the official who is entrusted with developing a plan for the street is quite conscientious and takes the findings of his questionnaire seriously. The plan he comes up with does amalgamate as far as possible the various conflicting preferences the residents have expressed. So judging on the basis of preference satisfaction, it isn't immediately obvious that self-determination must produce a better outcome. But now consider what might happen in an open discussion between the residents. People are likely to learn from one another, especially from people with particular expertise on relevant topics. Perhaps one neighbour is an engineer who can inform the residents about the effects of installing different kinds of speed bumps. Another might be able to talk about the kinds of trees that can be grown in large pots. Some of the ideas people initially had for improving the street might turn out to be non-starters on grounds like this.

The residents will also learn about one another's priorities. Some might have been hoping for an entirely pedestrianized street. But others who work some distance away say that they really do need to be able to park their cars near their homes. If discussion within the association works well, it can rule out solutions that some residents would find wholly unacceptable. What comes out at the end will be a compromise but one that everyone can live with. If we compare the self-determination alternative with the official alternative, we see that the former allows people not only to express preferences but to say how *strongly* they endorse or object to the proposals that are under discussion. Of course, the official could try to build strength indicators into his questionnaire ('How important is it to you that there should be play equipment in the street? Very/Quite/Somewhat/Not at all: Circle one'). But responses to such questions on paper aren't as revealing as having to defend your preferences in the face of objections, alternatives and cost constraints.

Those are reasons for thinking that the self-determination route will produce a better street design for the residents than even the most enlightened official enquiry. But there is another factor that may be equally, if not more, important. By forming an association, the street-dwellers are actively taking charge of their own immediate surroundings. They are constituting themselves as a group agent. At the end of their discussions, they will almost certainly have to persuade the local authority to help

implement their plans. We can imagine them author-
ising a delegation to go and make the argument on
their behalf. Even the residents who were not fully
in agreement with the final plan can feel a sense of
satisfaction if the proposal is accepted, or disap-
pointment if it is sent back. And when the road
scheme is eventually implemented, there is the
further satisfaction of looking down the enhanced
street and knowing that this is something they had
accomplished together. Because of the commitment
involved, it's more likely that the residents will feel
responsible for the upkeep of the plants and the
street furniture thereafter. This, then, reveals the
intrinsic value of collective self-determination: the
value of belonging to a group that can act so as to
make a difference to the world in accordance with
the formed will of its members.

We cannot expect everyone to attach the same
importance to exercising self-determination. Some
of the street's residents will find that they have
other priorities that prevent them from attending
street meetings. What matters is to have the opportunity to be involved, not to be compelled to do
so. Still, I need to say something to the person
who claims to find nothing to celebrate in self-
determination – who claims actually to prefer to
leave everything to the local bureaucrat. My reply is

that because we are socially embedded beings, not hermits, we have an interest in shaping our physical and social environment whether we recognize it or not. Lacking control, we risk experiencing our surroundings as alien and oppressive. If others with whom we identify exercise that control on our behalf, we might be lucky and avoid this sense of alienation, but it remains a gamble. I return in the next chapter to the question why *actual* control, and not just the vicarious feeling of being in control because we can identify with the people who are actually making the decisions, should matter to us. Now I want to consider how far the fable of the street can help to explain the value of self-determination for much larger groups, such as nations.

Critics of my story are likely to point out that it relied heavily on the direct involvement of the residents in the discussions that led to the final version of the scheme. Arguments were heard at first hand: child-free John came round to support including a play area after he heard the impassioned pleas of mother-of-three Judy. And a group identity was forged in the face of opposition from local bureaucrats whose objections had to be beaten down. But these processes surely cannot be transposed to groups numbering many millions. We will need to show how large impersonal groups like nations can organize themselves so as to enable their members to have a similar sense of active involvement in the group's trajectory, making self-determination not only instrumentally but also intrinsically valuable.

Before we move on from the street story, however, it is worth underlining four specific aspects that may be important for the argument ahead. First, the group that is created by the improvement project is not a wholly voluntary group. Of course, most residents will have chosen to live in the street, but that choice was likely made years ago and in no anticipation of the project in hand. What brings the group together is the unchosen fact that they are living in a street where people's quality of life is being seriously reduced by bothersome car drivers. So this is unlike the case of a self-selected group where every member joins precisely in order to carry out a predefined project and more like the case of a political community to which most members belong simply by virtue of birth and upbringing. We see that the value of group self-determination is not dependent on people having consented to join the group in question.

Second, it is also important that the group's membership is relatively stable over time. In a typical street, one or two houses will change hands each year, but most residents will stay put. This matters because in my story the same people were involved in the discussions and the ensuing to-and-fro with the local authority. For a broad consensus to emerge on what the redesigned street should look like, the participants should all listen to the same arguments and respect decisions taken at previous meetings. Moreover, the street redesign is a project that will take time to carry out, and its benefits will be felt later on, including by children as yet unborn. People are unlikely to commit to it unless they anticipate staying in the street for a few more years at least.

Third, there must be some basic level of agreement among the group at the outset if the process of self-determination is to get under way. In the case we're considering, that might just be a conviction that 'something must be done', given that life for people living in the street is currently quite unpleasant. This leaves a wide range of options open, but all of them will fall under the general heading of 'how to improve the quality of life for residents and their families'. That shared broad aim is what makes self-determination for the street-dwellers possible. Imagine instead that a significant minority of residents wanted to pursue the idea of turning the street into a drag-racing strip. Under those circumstances, self-determination for the whole group is impossible. Of course, a vote could be taken on their proposal, at which point the drag racers would lose, but that only reminds us that democracy (understood as a decision procedure) and self-determination are not the same. The drag racers cannot participate in the residents' evolving project so long as their only interest is in their diametrically opposed way of reconfiguring the street.

Fourth, self-determination is consistent with forms of representation whereby some people serve as spokespersons for the group as a whole, or are authorized to act in its name. In the street case, we might expect to see a committee forming to organize residents' meetings, and a delegation being chosen to conduct negotiations with the city. This does not detract from self-determination so long as the residents trust those who are to speak and act in their name and regard the final outcome as one that they have contributed to bringing about. Since self-determination on a large scale cannot avoid using systems of representation, it is worth stressing that this alone could not be the reason for rejecting national-level self-government as illusory.

So why think that the model of self-determination developed in the street example cannot be extended to much larger groups? The problem might appear to be that as we scale up, the actual impact that any individual can have on what the group does diminishes virtually to zero. As a resident, I can reasonably believe that when I spoke at a meeting in favour of including the tree planting, this actually helped to sway the group in that direction. But as a voter in an election or a referendum, my individual voice will make absolutely no difference to the overall result except in the most unlikely of cases, when the votes on either side are otherwise exactly balanced.

But why should individual impact matter so much? Sometimes it is important to contribute to collective projects even though one's own contribution is in reality wholly dispensable. Think of taking part in a demonstration, say a march against the use of fossil fuels, along with 100,000 others. It really makes no difference to the demonstration's impact whether you personally take part or not. And yet it may be very important to you to be there on that day, helping to achieve something to which you are strongly committed. Imagine someone stopping you from going and justifying this by pointing out that one additional demonstrator among 100,000 makes no practical difference. You would be deeply resentful of that person. And this reveals something about the way we understand ourselves as self-determining agents. We don't just think about the impact we have as separate individuals on our immediate surroundings; we also think about the impact on a much larger scale that we can have as members of groups we belong to and identify with. Nor is it irrational to care about this. 'What we did together' matters morally even in cases where my individual contribution to the collective result was minuscule.[6]

So scale alone is not a reason for denying the value of self-determination for large groups. But the example I gave to show this might be regarded as problematic because it assumes a single goal – banning the burning of fossil fuels – to which all the demonstrators are single-mindedly committed. And this is exceptional: in the political communities to which the right of self-determination is usually assigned, nation-states in other words, people are deeply divided on many of the issues that require a political decision, including the continued use of fossil fuels to generate energy. Even when majority voting is used to decide these questions, there seems no real sense in which the people as a whole enjoy self-determination. In other words, the political worlds we inhabit are much more like the divided street with its substantial minority of boy racers – or so critics of self-determination will allege. Beitz, for example, argues that the analogy often drawn between individual autonomy and state autonomy collapses for this reason: 'states, unlike persons, lack the unity of consciousness and the rational will that constitute the identity of persons. If states are not voluntary associations, neither are they organic wholes with the unity and integrity that attaches to persons qua persons.'[7]

The challenge, therefore, is to show that even large, diverse societies whose members are divided over many political issues can still function as group agents able to practise self-determination. There is one, historically famous, solution to this problem I will mention briefly, only to set it aside as unrealistic. This is Jean-Jacques Rousseau's theory of the general will.[8]

Rousseau's claim was when people were asked to decide some political question, such as whether a particular law should be passed, they would be unlikely initially to agree on an answer, and so they would have to assemble and take a vote. But he believed that so long as each person voted conscientiously, the verdict of the majority would express the general will. It would be *general* because those who had voted the other way would recognize that they were mistaken and would come to accept the decision as expressing their own real will. So when the decision was implemented, that would unequivocally be a case of self-determination for the whole group.

There are indeed cases in which, if you find yourself in a small minority on some question, it can be rational to conclude that you were mistaken and change your mind as a result.[9] But those will be cases in which everyone is trying to answer the same question, and there is agreement over what kind of evidence is relevant to the answer – questions such as whether a particular individual is guilty of the crime of which he is accused. But in so far as Rousseau was applying this logic to political issues, he was guilty of a kind of rationalist fallacy. He was failing to see that political disagreement very often arises from disagreement over underlying values, meaning that people diverge over what counts in favour and what counts against a particular decision. Under those circumstances, there cannot be a general will in Rousseau's sense – convergence on a proposal that everyone accepts as the right answer to the question being asked.

Instead, what may be possible in a large political community is widespread agreement on some very basic issues, coupled with substantial overlap in the reasons people see as relevant to deciding more specific questions. Each person is likely to weigh these reasons slightly differently, so there will be no perfect consensus, but when a decision is reached, people can see it as guided by reasons, most of which they recognize.[10] To make this clearer, return to the street example and notice how the self-determining street differs from the divided street with its minority of drag-racing fans. There is first of all universal agreement that the speeding traffic must be slowed. Then people will have different views about whether, for example, it's worth the cost of installing playground equipment. But virtually everyone agrees with the general aim of making the street more child-friendly, even though for some that's a more important objective than for others. In the case of the divided street, by contrast, we find completely different understandings of what the street should be *for* – so self-determination for the whole group of residents becomes impossible.

Self-determination through overlapping reasons requires an active public sphere in which issues are debated and people are exposed to the different arguments in favour of the laws and policies being considered for adoption. It's not enough just to be asked to cast a ballot from time to time since the bare act of voting reveals little about why a person has chosen to vote in one way rather than another. The public sphere includes all of the arenas in which ideas and argument are exchanged, from face-to-face discussions around the breakfast table and in the canteen through to internet blogs and the formal news media. What's important, from the perspective of self-determination, is that the public sphere should be inclusive and especially that it should not fracture into self-contained cliques inside which the members are only exposed to a restricted set of reasons not necessarily shared by those outside. This fracturing has become a very significant internal obstacle to self-determination in contemporary democracies. In the next chapter, we will need to examine how self-determining groups can be formed so as to discourage it.

Also reserved for the next chapter is a fuller discussion of the kind of decision-making procedure that a large group needs to use in order to be self-determining. In this one, I have been trying to bring out why, as individuals, we should care that the groups we belong to are autonomous. Although there is no direct path from personal autonomy to autonomy at group level, I have argued that when the group is constituted in the right way, we can value being involved in its projects, even though we only play a small causal role in bringing them to fruition. We can identify with those projects and take pleasure in their success. Of course, self-determination *can* be illusory when the group is effectively controlled by its leadership and members are given the feeling of participatory involvement without the reality: there are Nazi parades as well as people's marches. So more needs to be said about the conditions under which it is real.

3

The Agents of Self-Determination

I began this book by noticing that, in international law, the right to self-determination was attributed to 'peoples' without any further explanation of who was qualified to be one. In practice, a 'people' was understood to mean the citizens of an already established state, except in the case of the subjects of far-flung empires, who were entitled to create states of their own. But without in any way diminishing the importance of such cases, it still feels arbitrary to say that it is only groups fitting this description who have a valid claim to determine their own future. Why not minority nations like the Kurds, the Catalans or the Scots? Why not indigenous groups? Why not cities or regions? We need some principled reason for extending self-determination rights to some groups and denying them to others.

As a result of chapter 2, we should now have a better sense of why self-determination is valuable. That can help us to work out who can qualify as an agent of self-determination because a group that cannot realize its value has no defensible claim to it. Setting aside for now self-determination conflicts that may arise *between* groups, what must a group be like in order to have such a claim? Here are three features that appear to be necessary:

1 The group must have an identifiable membership. There must be widespread agreement on who counts as a member and who doesn't. It should be fairly obvious why. Self-determination must involve each member of the group having the opportunity to contribute in some way to what the group decides and does. If there were radical disagreement about who belongs to the group, it would be impossible to decide who should be allowed to take part in its decision procedures. A little uncertainty can be tolerated – if we think of the street example from chapter 2, we can imagine the residents debating whether temporary lodgers should be included in their discussions – but not much.

2 The composition of the group must remain reasonably stable over time. The reasons for this

were again foreshadowed in the last chapter. To have a value, self-determination must involve the group pursuing coherent policies whose effects they can see unfolding. The group that decides at one time must be largely the same as the group that experiences the effects of those decisions at some later time. Of course, there can be value in making collective decisions whose effects are instantaneous democratically. A touring theatre company may invite its audience each evening to select which play is to be performed, as the Globe players in the United Kingdom did in the summer of 2018 (three Shakespeare plays were on offer). This, presumably, maximizes playgoer satisfaction on the night, but it does not turn the audience into a self-determining group on the view I am presenting. There is no project that they are pursuing together, no continuing 'self' that takes responsibility for the consequences of the decisions it takes.

3 The group must have some procedure for taking and carrying out its decisions. Strictly speaking, it does not have to be formally organized, but a group without any organizational structure could hardly be self-determining unless it is very small and operates by members directly communicating their intentions to one another. A group

that acts together is not simply a group whose individual members happen to have similar aims and therefore behave in similar ways. There must be a coordinating mechanism even if it does not consist of a formal procedure like voting.

These three conditions for *group agency*, and therefore for the possibility of self-determination, are necessary but not yet sufficient. To see what else is needed, I want to make critical use of a contrast that Jeremy Waldron has drawn between *territorial* and *identity-based* conceptions of self-determination.[1] Waldron argues in favour of the former. On this view, any territorially concentrated group of people can qualify as an agent of self-determination. Following Kant, he defends 'the principle of proximity', according to which people who are unavoidably living side by side (and therefore liable to come into conflict with one another in the absence of a legal regime) are morally obliged to create a political authority to govern themselves, while having the right to decide on its constitution. In forming such a self-determining group, neither individual consent – since everyone resident in the relevant geographical area can be compelled to join – nor pre-existing cultural affinities between the members are to be taken into consideration.

This view of self-determination has some obvious attractions. By taking geographical proximity, together with willingness to collaborate politically, as sufficient to form a group agent for purposes of self-determination, it places no constraints on cultural or ideological diversity inside the group. People can hold entirely opposed beliefs and preferences on all kinds of subjects, and yet still (so it is claimed) engage in self-determination together. Indeed, the street example from chapter 2 seems to bear out Waldron's territorial conception. The residents formed themselves into a self-determining group simply on the basis of physical proximity, their unavoidable sharing of the space of the street. But before moving directly from the example to much larger groups, we should take note of two of its special features. First, the residents made themselves into a self-determining group for a specific purpose – the improvement of the street – rather than comprehensively. In other walks of life – their places of work, the schools their children attend, the sports clubs they join, and so forth – there is no need for them to interact and reach collective decisions. They can hold radically different opinions in these other spheres without this necessarily affecting their ability to reach agreement on how the architecture of the street should be redesigned.

So the conditions for achieving (genuine) self-determination are much less demanding than they might otherwise be because of its narrow scope. Second, because the residents interact directly with one another, it is much easier for them to develop the interpersonal trust that is necessary in order to reach compromises and to identify with the final plan that emerges.

Since Waldron intends the territorial conception to apply to political communities as large as modern states, he needs to show how mere geographical proximity can form a sufficient basis for self-determination in these cases too. Here he has to confront several difficulties.[2] One is that it is hard to understand why self-determination should be so important for a political community consti-tuted simply on this basis and nothing else. We can see why a geographically proximate group of people needs some mechanism to resolve disputes among its members, but it's not clear why an externally imposed system of law should not do the job equally well. Waldron has some difficulty in showing why a benign colonial regime wouldn't be an acceptable solution to the core problem of resolving social conflict that he identifies.[3] Another objection is that Waldron portrays the members of territorial communities as separate individuals with potentially conflicting interests and proposes a legal system with a democratic foundation as the preferred institutional mechanism for resolving these conflicts. But suppose instead that interspersed across the territory are two rival ethnic groups of unequal size. Then, instead of a neutral set of legal rules for conflict resolution, we should expect a regime tailored to the interests of the majority group to emerge. Why should the minority regard such a regime as a legitimate vehicle of self-determination? By way of illustration, consider the one-state solution sometimes proposed to resolve the Israeli–Palestinian conflict. Even if it were possible to create such a state, it would be incapable of delivering inclusive self-determination for the whole population; at best, it might be a vehicle for self-determination for whichever of the two groups – Jews or Palestinian Arabs – formed the majority at any time and was therefore able to assume control of the state's institutions.[4]

Let's turn therefore to the alternative view that Waldron rejects: the *identity-based* conception of self-determination. This holds that a self-determining group must be composed of members who share an identity that is more than just the fact of physical proximity. They believe they belong together because of features that distinguish them from members of other groups. The relevant features – which might be shared beliefs, shared experiences, shared commitments to future projects, and so on – will vary from one case to the next. In general, identity groups don't need to be territorially compact. A faith community, for example, can have members who are scattered across the globe. But if we are thinking about political self-determination, the group is also likely to have a physical space over which it wants to exercise control (whether there can be non-spatial forms of political self-determination is an issue we will return to in chapter 5). In other words, it will have a territory, even though it is not the mere fact of living there that defines the group.

The examples of identity-based political groups we are most familiar with are nations. These are groups whose members distinguish themselves from other peoples on political and/or cultural grounds, who think of themselves as having a shared history that they hope and intend will continue long into the future and a geographical homeland that they regard as the nation's own. So territory matters to nations but not just as a space in which group members can live in close proximity to one another. It is also seen as the repository of the group's past history and its culture, with sacred sites, monuments, quintessential landscapes, and so forth. This is why nations always resent territorial loss so deeply – and also why territorial conflicts often pose intractable problems for self-determination, as rival nations demand the right to control territory that they see as essential to national self-determination: think of Crimea, Kashmir or Kosovo.

How does having a shared identity of this kind help a group to be self-determining? It does so first by giving the group a set of reference points to which appeal can be made when decisions are being taken. Certain things can be taken for granted because they occupy a central place in the group's history or culture. If language, for example, is one of the features that defines a nation, this immediately provides a reason to protect its integrity (though as the Icelandic example in chapter 1 revealed, whether the nation is able to do so in practice is another matter). Alternatively, there may have been a defining moment when fundamental values were expressed – a declaration of independence and/or the writing of a new constitution, for example. As the street case revealed, self-determination is impossible unless the group shares some basic aims, even if there is quite strong disagreement about the best way to carry them out. Then, second, identity-sharing is valuable because when people are bound to one another emotionally as well as for practical reasons, they will be more strongly motivated to find ways of dealing with potential conflicts that are acceptable to all of the members. We know from many empirical studies that there is a positive relationship between shared identity and interpersonal trust.[5] Trust in turn matters for self-determination because where people trust one another, they also have an incentive to remain trust*worthy*, and this means they are more likely to give sincere reasons for the policies they favour and to adhere to compromises that have to be made to resolve contested issues.

To sum up the discussion so far, I have not tried to claim that self-determination is only possible in groups whose members already share a common identity of one kind or another. What I *have* argued is that if we are contemplating self-determination in large-scale societies and across a wide range of issues such as typically arise in the political communities we are familiar with, then having a common identity markedly increases the chances of success – whereas the presence of opposing collective identities, as found for example in ethnically divided societies, strongly reduces it. So group identity, along with the other three features listed at the beginning of the chapter, is a factor that conduces to the creation of a group agent capable of self-determination, in some circumstances an essential one.

But now we must look more closely at feature 3, the requirement that a self-determining group needs some procedure for taking and carrying out decisions. How can the procedure ensure that each member feels involved in determining the group's future? Must everything be decided by popular vote, for example? That may sound unfeasible, on the large scale. In the last chapter, I used the street model to argue that self-determination for the whole group was consistent with some people being selected to speak and act on its behalf. But there the relationship between the group and those chosen to represent it was close and direct, whereas at the national level it is inevitably going to be more distant. Self-determination requires that the reasons that weigh with the general public should also be the reasons that guide decision making by representatives and officials, but how is that to be achieved?

To make further progress here, I am going to juxtapose two ways of understanding the relationship between the group as a whole and those who decide on its behalf, which I will label the *correspondence* view and the *control* view.

On the correspondence view, it is sufficient for the group to be self-determining that its collective decisions substantively reflect the opinions of the members, even if the members at large are not in control of the decision-making mechanism. To illustrate, suppose that decisions are taken on behalf of the group by a ruler who is recognized as having the authority to do so. The ruler is concerned to please his people so he conscientiously conducts opinion polls on all important questions, and makes his decisions on the basis of what the polls reveal. He is not, though, constrained to do this: were he to break with this practice, he would not be instantly deposed.

On the rival control view, the scenario just described does not count as one of genuine self-determination. The missing element is that the people are not actively in control of the decisions that are taken in the name of the group. Their opinions are certainly reflected in the decisions taken on their behalf but only in a roundabout way that relies on the ruler continuing to govern on the basis of opinion polls.

Why might we think that correspondence is not sufficient for self-determination, that control is needed too? We might be concerned that correspondence by itself is not sufficiently robust. If correspondence depends on the ruler's own beliefs about the exercise of his authority, then it is vulnerable to a change of heart on his part, which might be provoked by a sharp clash between his own interests and the opinions of his subjects. But this is consistent with saying that correspondence is sufficient for self-determination so long as it continues. If we believe it is essential for there to be control even when correspondence is secure, we must have a different concern in mind.

Where there is only correspondence, as in the benign ruler case, what is lacking is the active involvement of the people in ruling. The people in that example are like children with benevolent parents who anticipate their preferences and provide the children with what they want; the children, though, are never given the right to decide for themselves. But self-determination in its strongest sense must involve the active exercise of political power by the people. That was a salient feature of the street case and also of the fossil fuels demonstration case. Continuing with the latter, suppose that the government does indeed change its policy following the demonstration. All those who participated have then shared in a successful exercise of collective agency. There is a relevant difference here between welcoming the government's decision because it corresponds with your own views (a reaction that anyone opposed to fossil fuels might have) and believing that you yourself have accomplished something by taking part in a collective action that forced the government to rethink its policy.

Against this, it might be argued that in some cases surrogate agency is sufficient. Consider decolonization: think of a society that for a century or more has been governed by outsiders with cultural and political values at odds with those of most of its members. It achieves independence and is now ruled by members of the local elite. The system, let's suppose, is democratic only in name since the leadership of the governing party is able to rig elections quite effectively. Nevertheless, most people may now feel that they have gained self-determination. They identify with their rulers and are able to regard the decisions the rulers take as if they were decisions taken by the whole people, even though they don't have any real control over what is decided. We might wonder whether this is all that self-determination can actually mean in large societies – a sense that the direction the society takes is being controlled by people with whom you identify.

Nevertheless, to reduce self-determination to the *feeling* of being in control of your collective destiny by virtue of identifying yourself, on cultural or other grounds, with those who are actually in control seems to deprive it of a large part of its value. We can expose the limitations of such an account by asking the following question: if a people is self-determining, shouldn't they also be held responsible for whatever their state does, where being held responsible entails being liable for the harms they inflict on themselves or on others? If we apply that standard, it is implausible to suppose that mere identification with the ruling group is sufficient for self-determination. If most ordinary Zimbabweans did indeed regard President Mugabe as 'father of the nation', as has been alleged, does that mean that on that ground alone they should be held collectively responsible for the economic devastation his policies inflicted? To reach that conclusion, we would need to say more about Mugabe's relationship to his subjects: we would need to show, for example, that his authority depended at least in part on following policies for which they expressed support.[6] In other words, we would need to establish that there was bottom-up as well as top-down influence. So if we use assignments of responsibility as a litmus test for self-determination, we can see that mere identification with leaders is not sufficient for the latter.

There needs also to be some agency exercised by the group as a whole, in this case by Zimbabweans conditioning their support for Mugabe on the policies he adopts.

So I conclude that, for a group to be self-determining in the fullest sense, its members must actively control its collective decisions. But what kind of bottom-up control is actually feasible in the case of large groups such as nations? One possibility would be to allow the members to vote directly on all major issues, in other words to have a series of plebiscites that would set the direction of public policy. But there are several objections to this proposal. One is that there are important decisions – such as whether to join a common currency like the euro – that demand specialist knowledge which ordinary citizens cannot reasonably be asked to acquire. Another, which we have already encountered in chapter 1, is that plebiscites only give straightforward answers to political questions that take a 'yes/no' form. If there are only two options worth considering, a majority vote in favour of one of them can at least be treated as meaningful. But few political issues are as simple as that. Usually there is an array of possibilities to choose between, so either we face potential indeterminacy for the reasons that emerged in the case of the proposed second Brexit referendum or, if a simple majority vote is to be held, someone has to whittle down the list of candidates until only two remain. And this hands power to whoever is able to do the whittling down, to frame the question that appears on the voting paper – thereby frustrating everyone who rejects the choice that is being offered and wants to vote in favour of some further alternative. A third concern is that even in the case of a political decision that really is a two-way choice, some people may have a much greater stake in the outcome than others. Think, for example, of a popular vote to legalize abortion in which the votes of men and women are counted equally. It is a failing of plebiscites that they take no account of the strength of interest or preference on either side of the issue so a largely indifferent majority might decide a question against the strong wishes or convictions of a smaller minority.

Popular self-determination, therefore, should not be understood to mean government by referendum. Referendums certainly have their uses as a way of conferring legitimacy on proposed constitutional and major policy changes, but they are only as good as the political process that precedes and accompanies them. That process itself should take the form of widespread deliberation among citizens, which involves citizens listening to and responding to one another's beliefs, commitments and preferences and reaching conclusions that they can justify to their fellows. In cases where there are several options on the table, open discussion allows people to explore the reasons for choosing one rather than another. Where it turns out that the rival options are being favoured on different grounds, it may be possible to come up with innovative solutions that almost everyone will find acceptable, thereby avoiding the problems identified above with simple 'yes/no' voting. As I suggested at the end of the last chapter, this exchanging of political reasons can take place in a variety of informal settings, but, for concrete decisions, a formal procedure is also needed. The next question, then, is about the institutional structure that is most conducive to self-determination.

The structure we are most familiar with involves electing representatives who are supposed to convey the views of those who elected them to a legislating assembly which then deliberates and decides. Upward control over these representatives is exercised by the threat of losing their seats, which gives those elected an incentive to respond to and as far as possible synthesize the view of their constituents. However, we know that this control mechanism operates far from perfectly in practice. This is partly because representatives live separately from those they represent and so are in constant danger of losing touch with the issues that most concern the latter, becoming in effect a professional elite. It is also partly because they are susceptible to lobbying by corporate and other interest groups with a heavy stake in the questions the legislature is addressing. So it is worth contemplating a further proposal, one which introduces what are now often called 'deliberative mini-publics', alongside elected representatives.[7] These are small groups of citizens chosen to mirror the larger society along lines of age, gender, ethnicity, social class, and so forth, and brought together to discuss issues of current political concern, either locally or nationally. The idea is that their deliberations would be a microcosm of those of the whole society, were it possible for it to assemble in one place. Several variants of this idea – citizen juries, citizen assemblies, deliberative opinion polls – have been tried out in different countries. These experiments show that ordinary citizens, when provided with relevant information about the questions they are asked to decide, and having to justify their views to others in a deliberative setting where conflicting points of view are represented, are able to reach well-reasoned conclusions. This contrasts markedly with opinion polls of the usual kind, which simply record people's instant responses to questions to which they may have given little or no prior thought.

What role should democratic mini-publics play in decision making itself if we want to promote collective self-determination? It would not make sense to have one such body making decisions for the whole society, effectively displacing representative institutions. While citizen bodies meeting on a short-term basis may be able to provide general guidance on policy questions, they cannot be expected to have the technical expertise needed for many of the specific decisions that have to be taken in contemporary democracies. Another reason is that, were they given such a role, their members would unavoidably come under the same pressures from outside interests that are now liable to distort the judgement of elected representatives. They would be subject to lobbying, to financial inducements, and so forth, all of which run counter to the deliberative ideal of reaching decisions by examining evidence and listening to arguments on each side of the question under discussion.

Instead, their role might be one of supplementing and counterbalancing the other institutions of self-determination. They could, on the one hand, have a significant influence on public opinion more generally if both the conclusions they reached and the reasons that lay behind them were widely publicized. Those who lacked either the time or the inclination to become well informed themselves on specific issues might be willing to take their cue from a mini-public if they were convinced that its members were 'people like them' who had simply explored the issue in greater depth. On the other hand, these citizen forums could serve as a check on representative institutions: where there was a marked discrepancy between the conclusions reached by a mini-public and by an elected body, this could signal that the latter had lost touch with the views of ordinary citizens. A parliament that legislated in defiance of the judgements reached after discussion in a well-informed citizen assembly would at the very least have to explain why it did so. In that sense, mini-publics within democracies might be able to exercise moral authority even if they were not given formal decision-making power.

We may still wonder how exactly creating institutions in which selected lay people are asked to adjudicate political issues directly contributes to self-determination. After all, the point about mini-publics is that very few people can actually

be included in them if they are to remain deliberative – citizen juries typically have twenty or
thirty members, citizen assemblies a hundred or so,
deliberative opinion polls twice that number.[8] The
chances of the average citizen being asked to join
one are therefore very low. So this is not a form of
mass political participation, and citizens at large
are not actively engaged in self-determination in
the same way as the residents in the street example
or the demonstrators in the fossil fuel example,
except on the rare occasions when they are invited
to vote for representatives. Critics will argue that
mini-publics may make a contribution to decision
making in local contexts, but at macro level there
is no substitute for informed participation among
citizens generally.[9] However, this argument fails to
explain how real deliberation, as opposed simply
to activism on the part of sectional groups, is
possible in a mass public in the absence of institutions intended to promote such deliberation,
with partisans being forced to confront rival views
and give reasons to justify their positions. There
undoubtedly have to be representative institutions
that can take authoritative decisions on behalf of
the people; it follows that, for the mass of citizens,
their involvement in collective political agency has
to be somewhat indirect. My claim has been that

self-determination at societal level will be enhanced when legislation and policy making are informally steered by the judgements arrived at in non-elite, non-specialist citizen forums.

Needless to say, all of this presupposes the value of self-determination at the higher level, as argued for in chapter 2. A sceptic may say that *real* self-determination can only happen on a small scale. But such a sceptic will need to explain why people should care so much about who is in control of their society to the extent that they are willing to break up well-functioning states in the name of national self-determination. The following chapter examines their reasons for doing so.

4

Self-Determination
and Secession

No discussion of self-determination can avoid
confronting its politically most disruptive
expression, namely the demand that an established state should be split apart in order to allow
one of its component parts to go it alone as an
independent state. This is the issue of secession.
The opposite case – combining two (or even more)
states to enable their united population to be self-
determining – happens much less often and raises
fewer issues since there is likely to be widespread
consent from both parties to the union: think of
East and West Germany joining together in 1990,
or the protracted creation of present day Canada
from its component provinces, beginning with the
British North America Act of 1867. Secession, by
contrast, is nearly always controversial, disputed
within both the community that aims to leave and

the rest of the state from which it is trying to escape. There are a few examples of uncontested secessions, such as Norway's split with Sweden in 1905, where a virtually unanimous vote by Norwegians in favour of independence was swiftly accepted by the Swedish government. But in the case of most of today's states that were formed by secession, breaking free from the mother state involved a struggle that frequently turned violent: Ireland from Great Britain, Bangladesh from Pakistan, Croatia and Bosnia from Yugoslavia, Eritrea from Ethiopia, East Timor from Indonesia – the list is long. Moreover, it does not include unsuccessful attempts at secession, such as Biafra's attempt to break away from Nigeria, or Tamil Eelam's from Sri Lanka, in the course of which many thousands of people were killed.

Many states today continue to house secessionist groups: most of these are non-violent, and many are small and relatively insignificant, but it is striking that several of the democratic states whose general performance would qualify them as highly successful by historical and comparative standards are nonetheless under serious threat of breaking up as the result of minority nationalism: most notably these include Belgium, Canada, Spain, and the United Kingdom. As I have already suggested, these are the cases in which we can most easily detect the pure force of the demand for self-determination since, in contrast to the experience of decolonization, the absence of democracy is not the main issue. But such demands are highly contentious, even if the effects of meeting them would be less calamitous than Robert Lansing feared.

Why is secession so controversial? There are a number of factors that make it so. One is that, like individual divorce, there has to be a division of the spoils. The accumulated assets of the state that is breaking up have to be shared between the two sides – the leavers and the remainers – and there is no self-evident formula for doing this fairly. Each side is likely to argue that it has contributed proportionately more than the other to the country's current prosperity or to make exclusive ownership claims to the valuable resources found in its part of the territory (as Scottish nationalists often did when North Sea oil was still flowing freely).

A second factor is that, unlike the Norwegian case referred to above, it is rare for support for secession to be almost unanimous.[1] It is much more likely that, if achieved at all, it will be achieved with the support of a narrow majority in the relevant area, as recent (unsuccessful) independence referendums in Catalonia, Scotland and Quebec indicate. Conversely, there will be a significant minority of people living within that region who are more or less strongly opposed to the split, either because they identify politically with the larger community in danger of being dismembered or because they have practical reasons – their jobs may be at risk, for example – for wishing it to remain intact. Indeed, taking the existing state as a whole, there may be many more people opposed to the secession than in favour of it, raising the question of who is legitimately entitled to decide whether it should go ahead.

Third, there is the thorny question of territory. How shall the boundaries of the seceding state be defined if the secession is to go ahead? If the decision to secede is made via a referendum, then it is usually assumed that the territory of the new state will coincide with the area in which the referendum is held. In practice, the relevant dividing lines are taken to be existing administrative boundaries: the Quebec that might one day become an independent state would be geographically identical to the existing Canadian province of that name.[2] But it isn't obvious that this is the right answer, particularly if we are viewing secession as a matter of self-determination. There might well be areas within those boundaries whose inhabitants would much prefer to stay part of the remainder state. When Quebec held an independence referendum in 1995, for example, several indigenous communities voted almost unanimously in favour of remaining part of Canada, believing that this would better protect their rights. Where boundaries could be adjusted to respect the wishes of groups such as these, it might seem this is what self-determination demands. However, the issue is complicated by the fact that both sides in a secessionist controversy are likely to have their own prior views about what rightfully belongs to their nation as its territory. I will look at this problem in greater detail below.

So when can a secession be justified, particularly secession from a state that is already democratic? If we turn to recent political philosophy for guidance, we can divide theories of secession into three main types. Following Wayne Norman, I shall refer to these as *just-cause theories*, *choice theories*, and *nationalist theories*.[3] Just-cause theories maintain that secession is only warranted when the seceding group is the victim of serious long-term injustice at the hands of the state it wishes to leave. Secession in these circumstances is remedial in nature: by establishing its own state, the group hopes to escape the injustice from which it has suffered up to now. Choice theories, in contrast, hold that any territorially concentrated group within the state is entitled to secede so long as it can show (for example, by holding a referendum in the relevant area) that its members want to be independent. Secession is seen here as a voluntary choice made by individuals who wish to withdraw their consent from the present state and by mutual agreement found a new one. Nationalist theories, finally, claim that any nation whose right of self-determination is thwarted by current political arrangements is entitled to break free and reconstitute itself as an independent state. Here what justifies secession is the desire of a group to express its collective identity and distinctive cultural or political values through becoming a self-governing political community.

These theories obviously provide very different ways of evaluating the claims made by secessionists. I want to look at them more closely through the lens of self-determination, starting with the just-cause theory, whose most prominent defender is Allen Buchanan.[4]

Over time, Buchanan has formulated his theory in slightly different ways, but the underlying thread is that an aspiring secessionist group must show that it has been the victim of serious injustice, while at the same time offering guarantees that the state it intends to establish would not simply replicate the injustice in the way that it treats its own internal minorities. What counts as injustice for this purpose? Buchanan lists three main cases: (a) large-scale and persistent violations of basic human rights; (b) the unjust taking of a legitimate state's territory; and (c) serious and persistent violations of an intra-state autonomy agreement. To give concrete illustrations, on Buchanan's account, Kurds who were subject to gas attacks by Saddam Hussein's Iraq would have the right to secede under clause (a). Estonians whose territory was incorporated into the Soviet Union against their will would be entitled to regain their independence under clause (b). And if the government of the United Kingdom were to remove all devolved powers from the Scottish parliament and rule Scotland directly from Westminster, Scots would have the right to break away under clause (c).

What Buchanan denies, on the other hand, is that the mere wish for independence on the part of a minority group, however strongly felt, can give them the right to demand it. He acknowledges the possibility of a consensual, Norway–Sweden style, secession in the absence of injustice, but in all other cases a justice-based reason must be given – and merely to refuse a widely supported self-determination claim does not qualify in his eyes as injustice. It might then appear that Buchanan simply fails to recognize the value of self-determination, but this is not so. Indeed, one of his main arguments for limiting the right to secede appeals to the self-determination rights of the people whose territory is under threat of being dismembered. The state's territorial integrity, he says, must be preserved not only to protect the existing rights and legitimate expectations of its citizens but also to allow them to practise self-determination over time. As he puts it: 'where the principle of territorial integrity is supported, citizens can generally proceed on the assumption that they and their children and perhaps their children's children will be subject to laws that are made through the same processes to which they are now subject – and whose quality they can influence by the character of their participation.'[5] So unless the secessionists can establish a rival territorial claim that is strong enough to defeat this principle – and that involves producing evidence of serious injustice to undermine the current state's legitimacy – citizens are entitled to reject their demands.

Buchanan's support of self-determination seems curiously one-sided, however. The state's citizens taken together are awarded self-determination rights, whereas the secessionists as a separate group are denied them. Apart from a concern to avoid the practical disruption that secession inevitably creates, the two groups seem to differ only in so far as the citizen body already possesses these rights and has a reasonable expectation that they will continue to do so, while the secessionists do not. But is this bias towards the status quo sufficient to justify the one-sidedness? Notice also that if the secession goes ahead, members of the remainder state still have the opportunity to be self-determining, though within a narrower compass. When southern Ireland (initially the Irish Free State) broke with the United Kingdom in 1922, this did not prevent UK citizens from continuing to practise self-determination over most of the things that mattered to them.

Another curiosity in Buchanan's view is that while he regards 'serious and persistent violations of an intra-state autonomy agreement' as an injustice for which secession may be a justifiable remedy, he does not see failing to establish autonomous institutions to allow minority self-determination as itself an injustice of the same kind. In other words, if your group's self-governance institutions are taken away or emasculated, you are entitled to secede, but not if the state refuses to create such institutions in the first place. Buchanan in fact strongly endorses intra-state autonomy regimes, especially for indigenous groups, but he does so on the grounds that they may be necessary to protect the individual human rights of group members. He doesn't allow that the interest in self-determination itself – a group's wish to shape its own social practices or to protect and develop its culture – could be strong enough that failing to recognize it would be unjust even if the rights of individual members are not at risk. And this means that his theory doesn't chime with the forces that in the real world impel minority groups to demand the right to secede or, falling short of that, to demand a substantial degree of autonomy within the state – a sense of their own distinctness from the majority and a wish to preserve it. That isn't a fatal objection to a normative theory, but it does suggest that we should look elsewhere for a theory of secession that can help to guide legal and political practice.

Let me turn, therefore, to the choice theory, which does indeed make the desire of group members for their own collective freedom the paramount factor justifying secession.[6] To recall, on this view any group within a state is entitled to secede if it can demonstrate that its claim is supported by a majority in a suitably demarcated area. The group does not have to be a minority nation or enjoy indigenous or any other special status. However, for the sake of consistency, the seceding group must also permit a minority *within* its chosen area the opportunity to carve out its own independent precinct, again by majority vote, and these independents could also decide to reconnect their territory to the original state (something on these lines might have happened had Scotland voted to leave the United Kingdom in 2014, whereupon the Shetland Islanders might have voted either to rejoin the United Kingdom or to become a self-governing territory). The underlying principle at work here is individual consent: self-determination must also involve the freedom to decide who your partners in self-governance will be.

The choice theory might seem vulnerable to the criticism that it permits endless fragmentation of the political community, as ever-smaller dissatisfied minorities demand the right to separate from the statelets they now inhabit. However, defenders of the choice theory may add a rider to the effect that a seceding group must be able to demonstrate that the political unit they are about to create can adequately discharge the functions that a state needs to perform in order to be legitimate, such as maintaining a viable economy and an effective system of law. This, they argue, serves as a barrier to fragmentation. Other conditions can also be added. For example, Harry Beran, in his defence of the choice theory, proposes that the new state should not form an enclave within the parent state, nor should it occupy an area that is 'culturally, economically or militarily essential to the existing state'.[7] These conditions taken by themselves may seem perfectly reasonable. But they raise two problems for the choice theory.

The first is that secession is not the same as collective emigration: secessionists are not like the Pilgrim Fathers who set sail in their quest for a new life carrying only their personal possessions. Crucially, it involves the taking of territory from the parent state – the area of land within which the vote to secede has occurred. So the secessionists have not only to demonstrate their determination to form a state of their own; they have also to prove that they are entitled to govern the territory over which their state will have jurisdiction, including all the resources that the territory contains, since under international law any legitimate state is entitled to dispose of the resources that lie on (or under) its territory. But how can merely being present together in one place at the moment at which an independence referendum is held create such a terri-torial entitlement? We can dramatize the point by imagining secessionists who encourage all of their supporters to move to a particular district and then promptly hold their referendum there. The problem is tacitly recognized by Beran when he concedes that secessionists cannot establish their state on a portion of land that is essential to the interests of the remainder state.

Equally, if not more important, is the concern that secession is never likely to result in the creation of politically homogeneous states in which everyone finds themselves associating with the partners they would most like to have. Instead, one majority–minority state will be replaced by two (or more) others. For instance, when largely Catholic Ireland seceded from the United Kingdom, it carried with it a large number of Protestants, nearly all of whom would have preferred to remain British; and when the Protestants who occupied the six counties of Northern Ireland resisted the break by fighting to remain part of the United Kingdom, they also took with them a very substantial minority of Catholics who came to resent the way the Protestants were treating them. No way of dividing the island into independent political communities could ensure that everyone's self-determination claims were adequately respected.

This brings us back to an issue touched on in earlier chapters: if self-determination is going to be feasible, it cannot depend upon people being able to choose all their partners in self-governance. On the contrary, a self-determining group is one whose members are able to resolve their disagreements and conflicting preferences and arrive at decisions that all the members can regard as reasonable and acceptable, even though some of them might secretly wish that other members would disappear from the scene. Very deep divisions within a society may make it impossible to achieve this goal (recall the divided street with its boy racers). But in that case splitting up the society may not help, unless its two segments are heavily concentrated in particular areas, in which case the number of people effectively excluded from self-determination is at least minimized.

In practical terms, the third theory of secession to be considered here – the nationalist theory – occupies a position intermediate between the first two.[8] It is more permissive of secession than the just-cause theory but less permissive than the choice theory because, as its name implies, it restricts the right to secede to groups that qualify as nations. Its core claim is that nations that cannot enjoy an adequate measure of self-determination unless they have their own state are entitled to secede from the state or states in which they are currently embedded. In rare cases, this could mean minority groups from several states combining to form a new one (the Kurds, who are currently dispersed across four states in the Middle East, provide an example). More often, it involves one province or region within an existing state, most of whose inhabitants share a national identity different from that of the majority within the state as a whole, claiming the right to become independent. The secessions that I listed at the beginning of this chapter all took that form. So the nationalist theory has at least the realistic virtue of identifying the cause that has actually led peoples to demand their independence. But what about its normative credentials?

The nationalist theory has some strong points in its favour. First, the quest for self-determination is built in to the very idea of being a nation. Nations are trans-historical communities. Being a member involves not just identifying with your present-day compatriots but with their predecessors, their actions, achievements and failures, and also with future generations, who it is hoped will carry forward the national project. What we, the people, decide now will significantly affect those future people – not only future compatriots, of course, but mainly those. So it is important that the decision-making 'we' should be the right 'we' – people who have the interests and anticipated values of our successors at heart. This link between identity and self-determination is one factor that distinguishes nations from groups of other kinds, for whom being self-governing may or may not matter, depending on the circumstances. For the residential street discussed in chapter 2, self-determination became important once the members recognized that only by acting together could they improve their environment. Yet, in another street not assailed by polluting cars, neighbours may be happy to interact socially without feeling the need to act collectively at all.

Second, people who share a national identity often have a strong concern that the identity itself, and the culture that goes with it, should be sustained. For example, they may fear the loss of a national language or of art forms like cinema that disappear not because anyone intends them to but because individual members have an economic incentive to behave in ways that erode these features. It may be personally rational, for example, to raise your children to speak a global language like English, or if you are a film director to make films that are stripped of culturally specific references in order to appeal to an international audience. By virtue of the control they are able to exercise over institutions such as the education system and the public media, states can do a great deal to resist cultural erosion of this kind. To make sure that the state does indeed act in this way, the safest bet is for the nation to have a state of its own.

Third, nationhood provides a solution to the problem of territorial entitlement, which, as we saw, the choice theory struggled with. Seceding groups need to show that they have a better claim to the land that they take with them than does the state they are quitting. Leaving aside for the moment the complications that arise when territories contain people whose national identities overlap, the nation as a group can identify an area of the earth's surface that qualifies as its homeland, normally by virtue of long-standing occupation. As I have argued elsewhere, groups who live on the same piece of land for long historical periods typically endow that land with group-specific value – either material value in the form of building infrastructure or improving the productivity of the soil, or symbolic value in the form of endowing places with special religious, cultural or historical significance for the group.[9] This in turn gives them a strong claim to remain in that place and to reap the benefits that they and their ancestors have created by retaining effective control over the territory.

But now consider some problems facing the nationalist theory of secession. The first is that, in its crudest form, it assumes that nations are culturally homogeneous and territorially compact groups of people who single-mindedly identify themselves with one nation. In reality, however, this is rarely, if ever, the case. The Irish example already referred to shows this. On the one hand, national populations are intermingled on the ground; on the other, many people have multiple identities, so it is difficult to assign them exclusively to one nation or other. For example, many people with English and Scottish identities also think of themselves as British – Britain in this case stands as an encompassing nation whose territory comprises the whole of the island subdivided between England, Scotland and Wales. So secession for Scotland or Wales would also involve the taking of territory to which the British nation as a whole has a legitimate claim on the same historical grounds as these smaller nations – that is to say, occupying land over time and endowing it with value in the course of doing so. Some may conclude, therefore, that secession could only be justified if all parties consented to it – were Scotland, say, to become an independent state, the British people as a whole would first have to agree to relinquish their claim to the land in question. Many Scots would contest this, but they have then to show why the smaller nation should take precedence over the larger one as the relevant unit of territorial self-determination.

This is perhaps the largest obstacle that the nationalist theory confronts – showing why the choice of unit for self-determination purposes isn't merely arbitrary. But there are other problems too. In contrast to the just-cause theory, the nationalist theory does not insist that seceding nations should demonstrate that they are victims of injustice. So it permits secession in cases where the seceding group is materially better off, on average, than the group it leaves behind. If Catalonia achieved independence from Spain, this would provide an example since Catalonia is one of the richest regions of Spain and contributes disproportionately to its economy. The problem here, therefore, is one of distributive justice. Most states (including Spain) have internal mechanisms that transfer resources from their more affluent to their less affluent regions in the interests of social justice. So even if a seceding nation makes a transfer payment at the moment of independence, the longer-term effect of splitting up will be to increase inequality between the secessionists and the remainder state. Self-determination and distributive justice appear to be at loggerheads.

Taking these two issues – multiple identities and distributive justice – together, the onus may be on the nationalists to show why the self-determination they seek cannot be achieved through autonomy arrangements within the existing state rather than outright secession. By creating devolved institutions such as the Catalan and Scottish parliaments, the smaller nations can be given control over many of the policy areas that concern them, while regional redistribution in the name of social justice continues and the self-determination rights of the larger nations in which they are embedded are also preserved, since many other questions will continue to be decided at state level. The nationalists themselves may want more than this, but is their claim a legitimate one, even in their own terms?

The major advantage that the nationalist theory has over its rivals, then, is that it does a good job of identifying groups that have especially strong claims to self-determination – it can explain why nations are 'special' in this respect. But it does a less good job of showing why these claims necessitate the nation having its own sovereign state, especially when the nation in question is already encapsulated in a well-functioning democracy. A demand for independence in these circumstances would be justified only if the state refused to create significant autonomy arrangements for its national minorities or if, having agreed to create them, it subsequently violated the agreement (for example, by repeatedly overriding legislation that lay within the competence of a devolved parliament). In addition, the seceding nation would need to show that it was indeed viable as an independent political unit. That would mean first of all establishing its entitlement to the territory over which its new state would exercise jurisdiction and then showing that it would be independent in reality as well as in name. A state that is so small and vulnerable that it will inevitably be dominated by a powerful neighbour cannot be presented as a potential vehicle of self-determination.[10]

The nationalist theory, therefore, turns out to be much less supportive of outright secession than one might initially assume. But is this a strike against it? I began the chapter by observing that secession is often presented as the paradigm case of self-determination. But this can easily backfire. Critics of secession, echoing Lansing, argue that rather than the creation of new states resolving conflicts, especially conflicts between rival ethnic groups, it tends instead to exacerbate them.[11] The group that wishes to secede has to sharpen the differences between its members and their neighbours in order to justify its independence claim; but if the secession then goes ahead, this can poison relations between the majority group in the new state and those trapped within it who have now become a minority, as happened, for example, in the case of Sikhs and Hindus in Pakistan or Serbs in Bosnia. The chance that post-secession states will become *inclusive* vehicles of self-determination may therefore often be slim. If so, we have reason to sever the apparently tight connection between self-determination and secession. Having a state of its own may, under certain conditions, be the preferred way for a group capable of self-determination to achieve it, but often there will be better alternatives available, even if self-determination is the only value at stake.

So, in the next chapter, we shall explore some of these alternatives. In particular, we will need to ask whether self-determination must always take a territorial form, or whether there might be groups with no specific territorial base that are able to practise it effectively. We have seen in this chapter how the desire for exclusive control over territory is often problematic for self-determination because of rivalries where two or more groups claim such control over the same piece of land. Sometimes, these conflicts can be resolved by dividing up territorial rights, as occurs when autonomy arrangements are put in place. How these might work needs to be explored in greater detail but so too does the possibility of new, geographically unbounded, forms of self-determination.

5

Self-Determination Within, Alongside and Beyond the Nation-State?

As the analysis in the last chapter revealed, we need to look more closely at the idea that self-determination, on a large scale, is best achieved through the institution of the nation-state. Secessionist groups buy into that idea. Their complaint is not about the state itself as an instrument of self-determination but about how state boundaries are currently drawn. Their number-one objective is to have a territorial state all of their own. But as we saw, this will often be hard to achieve without trapping minorities or inflicting injustice on other groups. The would-be secessionists may have to settle for something less, such as devolved government within one part of an existing state.

But is this necessarily a second-best solution? Why should we assume that a state is always the best institutional vehicle for self-determination? There are reasons to doubt this and to look instead for non-statist ways for groups to achieve an adequate measure of self-determination.

One important reason is that the capacity of states to act as their members want them to, even assuming widespread internal agreement, may be diminishing. We have touched on this problem already in chapter 1. The reasons have to do partly with interdependence between states and partly with the increasing complexity of the issues they have to confront. States have become heavily reliant on resources that are created outside of their borders in order to discharge their most basic functions, such as ensuring food supplies for their citizens, laying down and maintaining infra-structure, or running a public health service. So they have become embedded in elaborate networks of investment, trade and migration that cannot be disrupted without incurring significant costs. There is a price to be paid by states that try to reassert control over these networks, as negotia-tions over the United Kingdom's planned exit from the EU made only too clear. Not only did Britain turn out to be heavily reliant on migrant labour in sectors of the economy such as agriculture and house-building, but manufacturing industry had in many cases come to depend on the rapid and unrestricted supply of component parts across national boundaries.

The corollary that many would wish to draw is that, if self-determination is going to be a reality and not an illusion in the years ahead, it will have to be at a higher level – at European rather than national level, for example, or perhaps even at global level. A partial exception might be made for very large and powerful states, such as China and the United States, but otherwise, the critics claim, the territorial state as a vehicle of self-determination has had its day. It simply lacks the capacity to deliver the goals that its citizens might wish it to achieve.

But should we be looking upwards from the state in the search for new forms of self-determination? Why not downwards or sideways instead? Perhaps the best chance people have to engage in meaningful forms of self-determination is to organize locally around particular projects. After all, what matters most to people and has the greatest impact on their well-being is often what goes on in their immediate neighbourhood. This is also the arena in which people can most easily form themselves into group agents with internal means of communication that allow them to reach acceptable compromises, if not wholehearted consensus. The street model introduced in chapter 2 was, of course, fictitious, but it was meant to capture an already quite familiar form of local self-organization. The local community, then, even down to the level of a single street, might seem a promising candidate for self-determination rights.

Another small-scale arena in which self-determination might be both achievable and important is the workplace. For most people, a large part of their waking day is spent interacting with co-workers, but they typically have very little control over either the physical or the social aspects of their work environment. The major obstacle to self-determination here is, of course, the private ownership of workplaces, which allows owners and managers largely to dictate the terms and conditions under which people are employed in offices and factories. Some businesses do take the form of partnerships in which the employees can have a much greater say in the running of the firm since the management is ultimately answerable to them collectively. This raises the question of why employee-controlled firms are not the norm rather than the exception. Is it simply because workers are not in the end all that interested in self-determination at work provided their jobs are secure (and reasonably well-paid)? Or are there economic reasons why in a market economy in which most firms are privately owned, by individuals or shareholders, it is difficult for employee-owned firms to prosper, especially when it comes to obtaining the capital investment they need in order to develop? The issues here are too complex to be addressed in a limited space.[1] But we should at least remain open to the idea of changing financial and ownership rules in such a way as to make it easier for employee-controlled firms to be created, or for existing privately owned firms to convert themselves into partnerships, as John Spedan Lewis memorably did with the retail business that he owned and managed from the 1920s to the 1950s and that has since become one of the best-known groups of department stores and supermarkets in the United Kingdom.

Self-determination below the level of the state is also a major concern for cultural communities that are territorially compact but too small and/or too poorly resourced to be able to survive as independent states. Indigenous groups like those found in North America, Australasia and some parts of Europe are the best example (though in one respect an imperfect example since not all group members still live in its core territory).[2] These groups were once able to practise forms of self-government but were swallowed up, largely without their consent, by colonizing states. Self-determination remains valuable to them both for instrumental reasons – their culture and way of life remains somewhat distinct from that of the surrounding majority – and intrinsically – their members want to play an active role in shaping the group's future. But independence is not an option for them, even though some activists appear to hanker after it. Such groups are too dependent on the larger society in terms of economic viability and also for access to basic services like education and health care. So their self-determination has to take the form of *partial* self-government within the area identified as the group's territory, over matters such as property rights and support for language and culture that are seen as key to preserving the indigenous group as a distinct people.

What is noteworthy about each of these three types of groups – local communities, employees and indigenous peoples – is that although they are certainly capable of practising self-determination, the range of questions over which they can exercise their power of decision is relatively narrow. This is in marked contrast to political self-determination at state level, whose potential scope is very wide, extending to all those matters – lawmaking, public service provision, economic management, environmental protection, and so forth – that are legitimate concerns of the citizen body as a whole. Indeed, decision making at that level is especially important because of the way that these different issues interconnect, so a coherent policy that embraces them all is needed. This sets limits to small-scale self-determination within the state; decisions taken at local level have to fit in with state-wide public policy. Moreover, implementing these decisions usually requires resources that the state has to provide. Somebody has to pay for the speed bumps that will slow traffic through a residential street, and that somebody will almost certainly be a state-funded highway authority. As noted above, indigenous groups are also very likely to rely on various forms of state subsidy. This is not an argument against sub-state self-determination but a cautionary note about how much autonomy it is possible to achieve.

Like the nation-state, the groups discussed so far are all attached to specific places, even though it is not proximity alone that provides them with their identities: local residents have neighbourhoods, workers have offices and factories, indigenous groups have tribal lands. But is it essential for self-determination that it should be exercised by a geographically located group? It seems not. Associations often form among people who share a set of beliefs or a common interest, and such associations can have global reach: think of the Roman Catholic Church or the International Political Science Association. To become a member, a person only has to declare a commitment (and in the case of IPSA pay a fee); there are no territorial restrictions on belonging to the group. There seems no inherent reason why the members of such groups should not be collectively self-determining, though in practice many are not, either for practical or for doctrinal reasons (as in the case of the Catholic Church). But would self-determination in such cases always suffer from inbuilt limitations?

Let me explore the possible strengths and weaknesses of non-territorial forms of self-determination through an imaginary, though not entirely far-fetched, example. Manchester United Football Club claims to have more than 600 million fans worldwide, many of them in East Asia. Suppose this relationship was made more formal by reconstituting the Manchester United Supporters' Association so that any fan who wished to could join it, perhaps for a small fee. And suppose the Association became the owner of the club and its stadium, so the members collectively were in a position to make decisions about its running and its future. The internet would allow these members to exchange views about, and finally vote on, such questions – indeed the Manchester United Global App already exists so it would merely need to be repurposed for this to happen. The prospects for self-determination initially look bright. Many members of the fan base – the ones most likely to participate and vote – are passionate about the club. They almost certainly care more about its fate than they do about the political destinies of their states. They share an overriding interest in the footballing success of the club, thereby meeting one of the conditions laid down in chapter 3 for being a group agent capable of self-determination. We can imagine them voting on whether to keep or change the manager, who should be appointed team captain, which players should be on the priority list for new signings, and so forth.

So far, so good. But now consider some of the constraining factors. Although the members of the Association we are imagining can live anywhere, the club itself has a fixed territorial location. Old Trafford football stadium is situated in Sir Matt Busby Way, Manchester, and is thereby subject to English property law in general, as well as the more specific planning regulations of the Greater Manchester Authority. So any proposals to redevelop the stadium would need to be approved by the appropriate, territorially grounded, planning committee, whatever the fans might wish. Likewise, the employment contracts of the team and the management staff are regulated by English law and could not be varied by a vote of the fan base. Of course, the Club could decide to uproot itself and find another football ground in England or elsewhere, though at considerable cost in terms of loss of local support at its matches. Moreover, in order to remain in competition, it would need to comply with the rules of the English Premier League, as well as with the rules of the European club competitions such as the UEFA Champions League, which are now regarded as the ultimate testing grounds of footballing excellence. Thus many of the big decisions that the Supporters' Association might wish to take are in fact pre-empted by the laws and regulations of territorially based bodies, narrowing the scope of self-determination down to lesser decisions about personnel and other such matters within that framework.

The Association also suffers from a major internal weakness as a vehicle of self-determination: its inability to control its own membership. It is entirely reliant on self-identified supporters with benevolent intentions joining up and thereby acquiring participation rights. It cannot guarantee that the membership will remain stable over time. For example, the proportion of Chinese members might rise until they form a majority, and these members might then insist that the players should spend the summer break playing exhibition games in East Asia, to the distress of English and European fans who would prefer them to take a well-deserved holiday and be fresh for the new season. Nor is there anything to prevent supporters of rival clubs from conspiring to masquerade as Manchester United fans, joining the Association, and voting maliciously for incompetent managers and players.

This is a general failing of large-scale groups that rely on self-identification as the criterion of membership: there is no feasible way of distinguishing between potential members who genuinely share the group's aims and objectives and those who have other agendas. There may perhaps be (non-territorial) groups whose aims are such that no one other than a genuine fan would have any reason to join. If an international trainspotters' club were to form, it would very likely be protected from hostile incursions by the profound indifference of outsiders. But here the previous point recurs: there is not much of any substance that a voluntarily constituted trainspotters' club is able to decide.

The members can be self-determining, and indeed it would be wrong for any external body to prevent them from being so, but only across a very narrow scope and over matters that everyone *apart* from the members themselves would consider pretty trivial.[3]

Of course, these limitations reflect the fact that non-territorial associations have to operate in a world controlled by states, and so both the freedoms and the resources available to their members depend upon what various states are willing to grant them. We could perhaps imagine a world edging towards anarchy in which the scope of state authority shrinks and so more scope is left for such associations to exercise control over portions of their members' lives. Most visions of such a world, however, transfer the functions which the state now performs to the global market, and markets at best provide individual freedom of choice rather than collective self-determination (think of the internet or the big tech companies).

So, although territorial concentration alone is not enough to form people into a group agent capable of self-determination, for reasons spelt out in chapter 3, it seems that strong self-determination requires control over a territory where comprehensive decisions over the use of resources and other such matters can be made, as well as allowing membership of the group to be controlled. The next step, therefore, is to consider proposals for self-determination at territorial levels higher than the state – proposals motivated mainly by the observation that states are no longer self-sufficient political communities (if they ever were), while their decisions often have a major impact on communities and individuals outside of their borders. Membership of the self-determining collective needs to expand in response. But how is it possible to create the conditions for group agency at levels higher than the state? Even states, we saw in chapter 3, face problems as sites for self-determination by reason of their size and internal diversity, making it difficult for allegedly representative institutions to continue to reflect the aspirations of the people they are intended to serve. Such problems appear to multiply as we move to regional or global level.

For insight here, we can turn to the literature on global democracy, since it is hard to envisage how self-determination at these levels could be achieved except through democratic institutions of some kind.[4] So what are the prospects of such institutions being created? There are two broad paths we might follow. One is to attempt to create a democratic form of world government, with existing national democracies being converted into federated units under the auspices of a single authority elected by all the world's peoples. The other involves a more pluralistic arrangement with no single centre, whereby transnational democratic bodies, composed in different ways, would be responsible for taking decisions of particular kinds, say over the environment or international trade. This path is often referred to as 'global governance' to distinguish it from the first. Each path has its strengths and weaknesses, so let me review them briefly.[5]

The main strength of the world government path is that it promises to create an institution with the power and policy range of the state as we have it now, but at a level where it is able to deal with inherently transnational problems like war and climate change that bedevil existing states. The main problem it raises is to comprehend how such an institution could be democratic (and therefore a possible vehicle for self-determination) in anything other than the most formal of senses. Some advocates recommend the creation of a popularly elected global assembly to sit alongside the existing state-based United Nations General Assembly. But such a body would inevitably be very remote from the people who had voted for it. Constituency sizes would be huge: simple maths reveals that with a world population of seven billion, and an assembly with a thousand members – well above the normal size of democratic parliaments – each constituency would need to contain seven million voters. This means, of course, that many smaller states would have no single representative of their own: they would need to be bundled up with other small states. Even the fairly slender degree of contact that elected representatives in existing democracies manage to maintain with their constituents would be impossible to achieve under these circumstances.

Equally problematic are the internal dynamics of a body composed in this way. The United Nations as we know it is stymied by the conflicting interests of member states, which often prevent it from taking effective action even when the need for such action becomes obvious, as in the case of an impending genocide. As we know from chapter 3, an association that aspires to be self-determining needs a particular modus operandi. There has to be a basic level of agreement on what the association is intended to achieve, and beyond that the members must be willing to listen to the reasons for action put forward by others and be prepared to search for agreements and compromises that reflect the overall balance of opinion and interest in the group.

But, even leaving aside the fact that many states in today's world continue to be governed undemocratically, a global assembly would be so riven by differences of interest and ideology that it is hard to envisage how it could possibly function as a group agent of that kind. The decisions it reached would be determined by interest-based coalitions forming between representatives of a small number of powerful states.

One way to sum up the problem here is to say that democratic self-determination requires a demos – a body of people with the collective properties that would enable it to operate democratic institutions fairly and effectively – and there is little prospect of all of the world's peoples together forming such a demos. Of course, that might change with time, particularly if each of these peoples evolves its own stable form of democracy internally, so it would be unduly pessimistic to conclude that collective self-determination at global level will never be possible. But this must be a project for the far future, not for now.[6]

Consider next the global governance path to transnational self-determination. The proposal here is to democratize international organizations, so that people would gain control over the specific policies that affect their lives, such as financial regulation or the provision of development aid. The main problem, however, is deciding who should be counted as part of the demos that is entitled to exercise such control. Take an aid organization such as Oxfam as an example. If it is going to be made democratically accountable for how it decides to deploy its resources, we need to ask 'accountable to whom?' Perhaps democratic control should lie with the people who work in, fund and support the organization: they have created and sustained the organization for a purpose, in this case alleviating famine and global poverty, and should therefore decide how it carries out that aim. But, on the other hand, shouldn't control rest with those the organization is intended to serve – namely, the victims of famine and poverty whose interests are most severely affected by what the organization decides? It would be naive to think that the two sides will necessarily reach a consensus about how it should operate; indeed, it is even difficult to know who should be included in any such discussion – those whom Oxfam is currently helping or those it might help if it were to change its aid policies? Of course, it will usually be good practice for international organizations to consult the people whose lives are affected by their decisions. But this is very different from identifying a specific group whose right of self-determination extends to control over the aid organization that serves them.

Neither path to (meaningful) global democracy looks promising, therefore. We have to return to the nation-state as the institution that historically has enabled large-scale collective self-determination and that might take further steps to empower its own citizens along the lines proposed at the end of chapter 3. But we still have to face the problem that global forces of various kinds appear now to constrain the state's autonomy significantly. Is there any way for the nation-state to escape from these constraints?

I will explore the possibilities here by considering how one very small state, Iceland, responded to the challenges it faced as a result of the 2008 banking crisis, which saw the collapse of all four of the country's national banks.[7] The impact of this crisis was very severe: GDP fell by 10%, and disposable household incomes by 20%; the Icelandic krona lost 50% of its value and unemployment rose from 3% to 9% in a short space of time. So we might see this as a classic case of a country being brought to its knees by external factors after having chosen to adopt an economic growth policy that was heavily reliant on expanding its international banking sector. The more interesting phenomenon, however, is the Icelandic people's response to the crisis. A popular movement erupted – called the 'Pots and Pans' revolution because increasing numbers of citizens demonstrated outside parliament banging these as instruments to register their disgust with the way both the bankers and their supporters in government had behaved – leading finally to the election of a left-wing government with a very different policy agenda. Alongside this, a democratic mini-public was created in the shape of a national forum with around a thousand members, charged with articulating the values and priorities that Iceland should pursue in the future. A major issue was whether the country should adopt a new constitution. Alongside the larger forum, a smaller constitutional council was created which posted up drafts of the proposed new constitution as its deliberations proceeded, encouraging ordinary citizens to comment and integrating these comments into later drafts.[8] Although the final version eventually failed to win parliamentary approval, what is noteworthy is how in this case a major financial crisis brought people together to deliberate on their common future and to search for an institutional framework that would better enable them to pursue their aims. Meanwhile, the newly elected government pursued a radical economic policy that, rather than adopting austerity measures as many governments worldwide did following the 2008 crash, used government borrowing to stimulate the economy and introduced a strongly redistributive tax-and-welfare system to protect those on lower incomes from the effects of inflation. The effect, going forward, was that the Icelandic economy grew faster than any other western economy, unemployment was back down below 3 per cent by 2016 and income inequality was sharply diminished.[9]

The Icelandic case is surely exceptional – but it is exceptional in two contrasting ways. As a small state with a population of less than 350,000 occupying a territory with limited resources and heavily reliant on three main industries – tourism, fishing and aluminium smelting – for external earnings, it is starkly exposed to shifts in the global economy. But as its response to the crash shows, the solidarity of its citizens also allowed it to respond to a crisis through a radical change of policy, in the course of which higher earners were willing to take on additional tax burdens to protect their compatriots' living standards. What happened from 2009 onwards can be seen as a remarkable instance of popular self-determination. There was, understandably, also an inclination to look for external support: Icelanders began to rethink their long-held aversion to joining the European Union. But finally their choice was to preserve greater freedom of manoeuvre by remaining part of the looser European Free Trade Area alongside Norway and Switzerland, two other countries that illustrate how relatively small states can continue to preserve their autonomy despite being fully integrated into the global economy.

Critics will argue that we cannot generalize from these cases: there are special factors, internal and external, that allow these countries to pursue their own independent paths. But the lesson I want to draw is a different one, namely that people who value self-determination have to be willing to make sacrifices to achieve and/or preserve it. The Icelanders did this when they turned their backs on the get-rich-quick banking bonanza they had been indulging in during the mid-2000s. How big those sacrifices are will of course depend on where you begin from: a people being ruled from the outside may have to engage in a violent struggle to rid themselves of that domination, while for others it may only require taking economic losses to avoid having to comply with the rules of transnational bodies. So the normative question we must ask is whether such sacrifices are worth making. Can self-determination really be so important that people should be willing to part with their resources, their liberties and even their lives to realize it?

This takes us back to the questions raised at the beginning of chapter 2 about the value of self-determination. I argued there that it was wrong to treat collective autonomy as something that people in all times and places either actually valued or had reason to value. In other words, it is not a universal human value in the way that elementary justice is. Nonetheless, it is integral to the modern, post-Enlightenment, human condition. Although there may be circumstances in which the price of fighting for self-determination is simply too high – think of trying to resist the Chinese will to dominate Tibet – we cannot simply resign ourselves to being at the mercy of forces outside our control, whether the gods or international bankers. We need to take charge, and we have to do it together rather than as individuals (*very* rich people might think that they are entirely masters of their own fate, but in so far as this is true, it is only courtesy of the work of millions of others in providing the social conditions under which the super-rich can live their self-indulgent lives). But then the question is 'together with whom?', and in this chapter I have been looking at various possible arenas *other* than the nation-state in which self-determination might be practised. All, it turns out, have limitations as well as strengths. Our pursuit of collective autonomy must, therefore, take place in multiple domains from local communities and workplaces right up to the international bodies that serve our special interests. If nation-states still remain privileged from this perspective, it is because, at their best, they are able to provide the internal conditions under which their peoples can become effective group agents while retaining a sufficiently wide range of powers to make self-determination more than just a formality.

Self-determination is not, then, merely a dangerous illusion. It is something that all of us can and should aspire to be involved in. But we need to be realistic about the conditions under which genuine self-determination (rather than a bogus, elite-manipulated, version) is possible. My aim throughout the book has been to explore what these conditions are.

Notes

Chapter 1 Introduction

1 The UN has also on occasion attributed rights of determination to specific groups that do not fit easily into these categories, notably the Palestinians and the black population of apartheid South Africa. For a much fuller discussion of the different ways in which the term 'people' has been understood in international law, see T. Musgrave, *Self-Determination and National Minorities* (Oxford: Oxford University Press, 1997), ch. 7.

2 Cited in A. Cassese, *Self-Determination of Peoples: A Legal Reappraisal* (Cambridge: Cambridge University Press, 1995), p. 20.

3 R. Lansing, *The Peace Negotiations: A Personal Narrative* (London: Constable, 1921), p. 87.

4 *Uti possidetis*, meaning 'as you possess', originated as a doctrine in Roman law that stabilized property

by awarding continued possession of a disputed item to the current holder. It was later applied by analogy in international law to the territorial holdings of states.

5 See S. Ratner, 'Drawing a Better Line: *Uti Possidetis* and the Borders of New States', *American Journal of International Law* 90 (1996): 602–4; and M. Moore, 'The Territorial Dimension of Self-Determination', section 1, in M. Moore (ed.), *National Self–Determination and Secession* (Oxford: Oxford University Press, 1998), pp. 134–57.

6 According to a local speech pathologist, 'More and more often, children with little Icelandic comprehension are being referred to me. I'll show them pictures of commonplace objects and ask them to tell me the object's name. Often I'll receive answers such as: "I know what this is, I just don't know what it's called in Icelandic". When I ask whether they know the object's name in English, they're quick to reply.' https://icelandmag.is/article/icelandic-children-have-better-comprehension-english-icelandic-says-speech-pathologist.

7 I. Jennings, *The Approach to Self-Government* (Cambridge: Cambridge University Press, 1956), p. 56. See also F. Whelan, 'Prologue: Democratic Theory and the Boundary Problem', in J. R. Pennock and J. W. Chapman (eds), *Nomos XXV: Liberal Democracy* (New York: New York University Press, 1983).

8 See, for example, I. Somin, *Democracy and Political
   Ignorance* (Stanford, CA: Stanford University Press,
   2013); C. Achen and L. Bartels, *Democracy for
   Realists* (Princeton, NJ: Princeton University Press,
   2015).

9 For a critical appraisal, see A. Weale, *The Will of the
   People: A Modern Myth* (Cambridge: Polity Press,
   2018).

10 Readers who are familiar with voting theory will
   immediately recognize the problem that I am
   presenting informally here.

Chapter 2 The Value of Self-Determination

1 https://www.constitution.org/scot/arbroath.htm.

2 In doing so I join B. Barry, 'Self-Government Revisited',
   in D. Miller and L. Siedentop (eds), *The Nature of
   Political Theory* (Oxford: Clarendon Press, 1983), pp.
   121–54; and C. Wellman, *A Theory of Secession: The
   Case for Political Self-Determination* (Cambridge:
   Cambridge University Press, 2005), pp. 42–4.

3 This is the main thesis of S. Conly, *Against Autonomy:
   Justifying   Coercive   Paternalism*   (Cambridge:
   Cambridge University Press, 2013), who draws upon
   the evidence about human practical irrationality to
   defend paternalist policies that constrain people in
   their own best interests. The relevant evidence can
   be sampled in many places including R. Thaler and

C. Sunstein, *Nudge: Improving Decisions about Health, Wealth, and Happiness* (New Haven, CN: Yale University Press, 2008); and D. Kahneman, *Thinking Fast and Slow* (London: Penguin, 2012).

4 For a fuller statement of the argument that denying a group self-determination manifests a failure of respect for its members, see Wellman, *Theory of Secession*, pp. 55–8.

5 A similar strategy is adopted by Anna Stilz in 'The Value of Self-Determination', in D. Sobel, P. Vallentyne and S. Wall (eds), *Oxford Studies in Political Philosophy*, vol. 2 (Oxford: Oxford University Press, 2016), pp. 98–127, though her way of bridging between the small-group context and a large political community such as a state is different from mine.

6 On this, see D. Parfit, *Reasons and Persons* (Oxford: Clarendon Press, 1984), ch. 3; and R. Tuck, *Free Riding* (Cambridge, MA: Harvard University Press, 2008), ch. 2.

7 C. Beitz, *Political Theory and International Relations*, 2nd edn (Princeton, NJ: Princeton University Press, 1999), p. 81.

8 J.-J. Rousseau, *The Social Contract*, esp. Book IV, ch. 2 in J.-J. Rousseau, *The Social Contract and Other Later Political Writings*, trans. and ed. V. Gourevitch (Cambridge: Cambridge University Press, 1997). I am using Rousseau here to represent a particular view of how self-determination for large groups is possible. Others may read him differently. It is also

relevant that Rousseau explicitly intended his theory to apply only to small and relatively homogeneous societies, bemoaning 'the immensity of States' as one of the factors that prevented the general will from being heard (Book III, ch. 15).

9 Rousseau's near-contemporary, the Marquis de Condorcet, later presented the so-called 'jury theorem' which calculates the probability of a majority vote on some question yielding the correct answer, given the probability of each individual voter getting the answer right. As the number of voters increases, then provided that probability is higher than 50 per cent, the likelihood that the majority vote will be right rises to virtual certainty. For an accessible informal presentation of the theorem, see A. Weale, *The Will of the People: A Modern Myth* (Cambridge: Polity Press, 2018), ch. 6.

10 Political philosophers often now describe this as making decisions through the use of 'public reason'. For an overview of this concept, see J. Quong, 'On the Idea of Public Reason', in J. Mandle and D. Reidy (eds), *A Companion to Rawls* (Chichester: Wiley-Blackwell, 2014).

Chapter 3 The Agents of Self-Determination

1 J. Waldron, 'Two Conceptions of Self-Determination', in S. Besson and J. Tasioulas (eds), *The Philosophy*

of International Law (Oxford: Oxford University Press, 2010), pp. 397–413.

2 I draw here on my longer discussion of Waldron in D. Miller, 'Neo-Kantian Theories of Self-Determination: a Critique', *Review of International Studies* 42 (2016): 858–75.

3 See Waldron, 'Two Conceptions of Self-Determination', pp. 411–12.

4 I am simplifying the proposal here for purposes of illustration. Its proponents do not in fact advocate a unitary state but rather a complex federal arrangement in which each community is entrusted with substantial powers to organize its own collective life: see, for example, A. Burg, 'The One State Solution', *Prospect*, September 2018. Assuming this can be made to work, each community becomes partially self-determining. But there is still no significant sense in which the people of the land of Israel–Palestine could enjoy self-determination as a single people so long as they remain deeply divided ethnically and politically.

5 For an overview of the evidence, see P. Lenard and D. Miller, 'Trust and National Identity', in E. Uslaner (ed.), *The Oxford Handbook of Social and Political Trust* (Oxford: Oxford University Press, 2018).

6 I have discussed the problem of assigning collective responsibility in autocracies more fully in D. Miller, *National Responsibility and Global Justice* (Oxford: Oxford University Press, 2007), ch. 5.

7 See M. Setälä and G. Smith, 'Mini-Publics and Deliberative Democracy', in A. Bächtiger, J. Dryzek, J. Mansbridge and M. Warren (eds), *The Oxford Handbook of Deliberative Democracy* (Oxford: Oxford University Press, 2018); K. Grönlund, A. Bächtiger and M. Setälä (eds), *Deliberative Mini-Publics: Involving Citizens in the Democratic Process* (Colchester: ECPR Press, 2014).

8 See Setälä and Smith, 'Mini-Publics and Deliberative Democracy', p. 301.

9 See C. Lafont, 'Deliberation, Participation, and Democratic Legitimacy: Should Deliberative Mini-publics Shape Public Policy?', *Journal of Political Philosophy* 23 (2015): 40–63.

Chapter 4 Self-Determination and Secession

1 Here I am considering secession from an existing democratic state. There may be overwhelming support for breaking away from an empire like the Soviet Union in order to create one.

2 As noted earlier, international law does not recognize a right of secession, except in the special case of decolonization, but if secession does indeed occur, it must take place within existing administrative boundaries. For discussion, see S. Lalonde, *Determining Boundaries in a Conflicted World: the Role of* Uti Possidetis (Montreal and Kingston: McGill-Queen's

University Press, 2002); S. Ratner, 'Drawing a Better Line: *Uti Possidetis* and the Borders of New States', *American Journal of International Law* 90 (1996): 590–624.

3 See W. Norman, 'The Ethics of Secession as the Regulation of Secessionist Politics', in M. Moore (ed.), *National Self-Determination and Secession* (Oxford: Oxford University Press, 1998); W. Norman, 'Domesticating Secession' in S. Macedo and A. Buchanan (eds), *Nomos XLV: Secession and Self-Determination* (New York: New York University Press, 2003).

4 See especially A. Buchanan, *Secession: The Morality of Political Divorce from Fort Sumter to Lithuania and Quebec* (Boulder, CO: Westview Press, 1991); A. Buchanan, *Justice, Legitimacy, and Self-Determination* (Oxford: Oxford University Press, 2004), ch. 8. In his later work especially, Buchanan insists that his aim is to define a right to secede that might be recognized by international law, as opposed to what he calls 'a moral right to secede', but for present purposes I am going to bracket off this methodological issue.

5 A. Buchanan, 'Theories of Secession', *Philosophy and Public Affairs* 26 (1997): 31–61, esp. 47–8.

6 Prominent examples include H. Beran, 'A Liberal Theory of Secession', *Political Studies* 32 (1984): 21–31; C. Wellman, 'A Defense of Secession and Political Self-Determination', *Philosophy*

and Public Affairs 24 (1995): 142–71; D. Copp, 'Democracy and Communal Self-Determination', in R. McKim and J. McMahan (eds), *The Morality of Nationalism* (New York: Oxford University Press, 1997).

7 Beran, 'A Liberal Theory of Secession', pp. 30–1.

8 See D. Miller, 'Secession and the Principle of Nationality' and K. Nielsen, 'Liberal Nationalism and Secession', both in Moore (ed.), *National Self-Determination and Secession.*

9 D. Miller, 'Territorial Rights: Concept and Justification', *Political Studies* 60 (2012): 252–68.

10 This shows why secession may not always represent a gain for democracy, as nationalists might wish to claim. It's true that within a smaller political unit, citizens are more likely to exercise bottom-up control over their representatives. But this has to be set against the narrower set of policy options open to a small state, given the constraints imposed by its external environment. The classic study of this dilemma is R. Dahl and E. Tufte, *Size and Democracy* (Stanford, CA: Stanford University Press, 1974).

11 See, for example, D. Horowitz, 'Self-Determination: Politics, Philosophy, Law', in Moore (ed.), *National Self-Determination and Secession.*

Chapter 5 Self-Determination Within, Alongside and Beyond the Nation-State?

1 For a helpful overview, see G. Dow, *Governing the Firm: Workers' Control in Theory and Practice* (Cambridge: Cambridge University Press, 2003), esp. ch. 11. My own answer can be found in D. Miller, 'Market Neutrality and the Failure of Co-operatives', *British Journal of Political Science* 11 (1981): 309–29.

2 See the discussion in M. Moore, 'An Historical Argument for Indigenous Self-Determination', in S. Macedo and A. Buchanan (eds), *Nomos XLV: Secession and Self-Determination* (New York: New York University Press, 2003).

3 Churches provide a more serious example, though note that what protects them against incursion is their prior commitment to a body of beliefs and practices, which also restricts the scope of self-determination.

4 This literature is now very extensive. To sample it, see D. Held, *Democracy and the Global Order* (Cambridge: Polity Press, 1995); C. List and M. Koenig-Archibugi, 'Can There Be a Global Demos? An Agency-Based Approach', *Philosophy and Public Affairs* 38 (2010): 76–110; D. Archibugi, M. Koenig-Archibugi and R. Marchetti (eds), *Global Democracy: Normative and Empirical Perspectives* (Cambridge: Cambridge University Press, 2011); L.

Valentini, 'No Global Demos, No Global Democracy? A Systematisation and Critique', *Perspectives on Politics* 12 (2014): 789–807.

5 I draw here on my longer discussion in D. Miller, 'Against Global Democracy' in K. Breen and S. O'Neill (eds), *After the Nation: Critical Reflections on Post-Nationalism* (Basingstoke: Palgrave Macmillan, 2010).

6 See also the thoughtful discussion in Valentini, 'No Global Demos, No Global Democracy?'.

7 I rely in what follows on E. Bergmann, *Iceland and the International Financial Crisis: Boom, Bust and Recovery* (Basingstoke: Palgrave Macmillan, 2014); P. Urfalino, V. Ingimundarson and I. Erlingsdóttir (eds), *Iceland's Financial Crisis: The Politics of Blame, Protest, and Reconstruction* (London: Routledge, 2016); B. Thorhallsson (ed.), *Small States and Shelter Theory: Iceland's External Affairs* (London: Routledge, 2018).

8 For a full description and evaluation, see H. Landemore, 'Inclusive Constitution-Making: The Icelandic Experiment', *Journal of Political Philosophy* 23 (2015): 166–91.

9 The Gini co-efficient that measures income inequality fell by 18.9 per cent between 2008 and 2011. See S. Olafsson, 'The Strategy of Redistribution: Iceland's Way Out of the Crisis', in Urfalino et al., *Iceland's Financial Crisis.*